BASEBALL
Picture Quiz Book

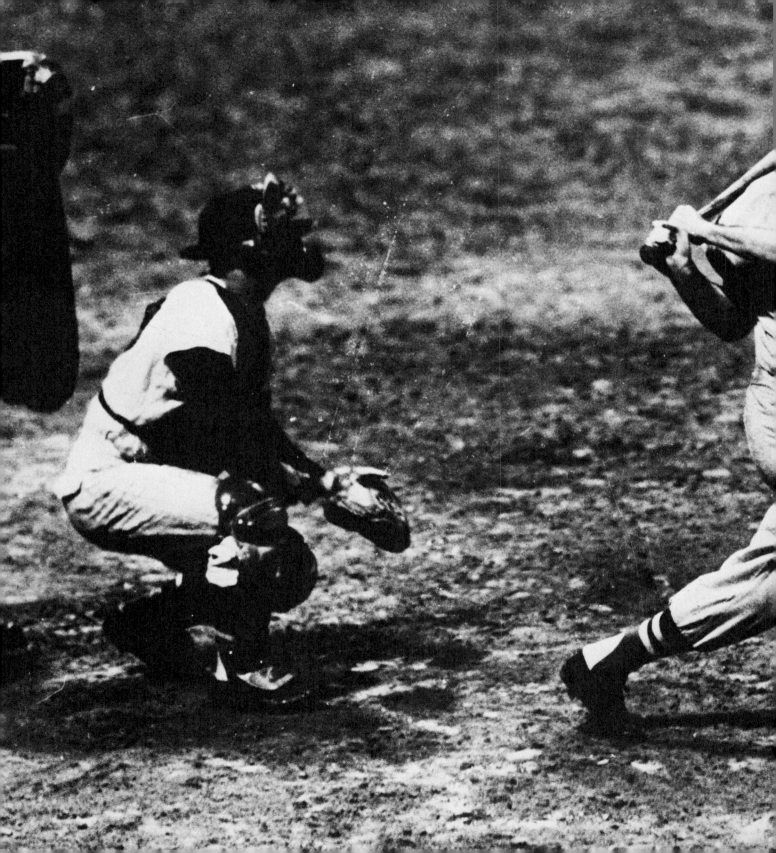

BASEBALL
Picture Quiz Book

Bert Randolph Sugar
&
John Grafton

Dover Publications, Inc.
New York

Published in Canada by General Publishing Company, Ltd., 30
Lesmill Road, Don Mills, Toronto, Ontario.
Published in the United Kingdom by Constable and Company,
Ltd., 10 Orange Street, London WC2H 7EG.

Baseball Picture Quiz Book is a new work, first published by
Dover Publications, Inc., in 1980.

Book design by Carol Belanger Grafton

International Standard Book Number: 0-486-23987-X
Library of Congress Catalog Card Number: 79-57040

Manufactured in the United States of America
Dover Publications, Inc.
180 Varick Street
New York, N.Y. 10014

PREFACE

Here are 220 photographs of some of baseball's greatest personalities from before the turn of the century right up to the present day. Keyed to each photograph are baseball questions which range from fairly easy to very difficult, and which the authors hope will prove entertaining to all, from the novice to the most expert baseball fan. The game of baseball "trivia" needs no introduction to its millions of devotees. We hope that even veteran practitioners of this sport-within-a-sport will find new material here on which to test their knowledge and sharpen their wits and we wish our readers as much fun in answering the questions as we have had in asking them.

With thanks to Mike Aronstein.

B.R.S.
J.G.

BASEBALL
Picture Quiz Book

1

2

3

1 & 2. The players pictured here are the only brothers in major league history to win a league batting championship each. The players in **3 & 4** are the only brothers who each hit a home run in All Star games. Identify them. There have been six sets of *twin* brothers to play in the major leagues; name the twins that played most recently.

4

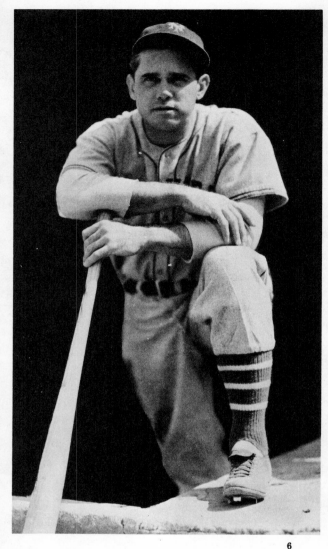

6

5 & 6. One of these players had the shortest career of any player to win just *one* league batting championship. The other had the highest batting average in his league-leading season of all 20th-century players who won just one batting championship. Name them.

7 & 8. The players pictured are two of the six men in major league history who played at least 20 seasons and won just one batting championship. Identify them. Name the other four.

9

11

10

9–11. Since the start of the 1939 season only five men have managed the Brooklyn–Los Angeles Dodgers. Name the three Dodger managers pictured on these pages, and the other two men who have led the club since 1939. One of these Dodger managers had a major league playing career that lasted for only one at bat, in 1936. However, only two men in major league history have managed one team longer. Name them.

12. Identify this Dodger right-hander. He played his entire 14-year career for one of these managers, longer than any other player who played a whole career under only one manager.

13

14

13. This Cincinnati outfielder once played in 508 consecutive games. Is this a record for National League outfielders? What is the major league record for most career home runs by a player who *never* led the league in runs batted in?

14. This National League slugger is one of three men in major league history to have over 6000 total bases. Name him and the other two men in this category. Which one had the highest career average?

15

15. This Pittsburgh Pirate is one of four National League players to hit at least three home runs in a game twice in one year. Name him and the other three. Who is the only American League player to do this?

16. This Hall of Fame member won more games than any other left-hander in major league history except one. Name him and the left-hander ahead of him on the all-time win list.

17. This Cleveland player, hit on the head by a pitch, is the only man to die as the result of an injury suffered in a major league game. Name him and the pitcher who threw the fatal pitch.

18 & 19. Identify these two pitchers who, a year apart, became the 18th and 19th men since 1900 to pitch and win two complete games on the same day. Who was the last pitcher to accomplish this rare feat?

20. Identify this left-hander who won 84 and lost 75 games during a major league career that began before the turn of the century. He is remembered today, however, for the records he set during his long tenure as a coach for the Washington Senators. Making a special late-season appearance as a pinch hitter in 1924, he became, at 48, the oldest man ever to hit a triple in the major leagues. In 1933, at 57, he became the oldest man to appear, up to that time, in a major league game, a record which was broken in 1965 by the pitcher in **21**, who can also claim the distinction of being the first black pitcher in the American League. Name him.

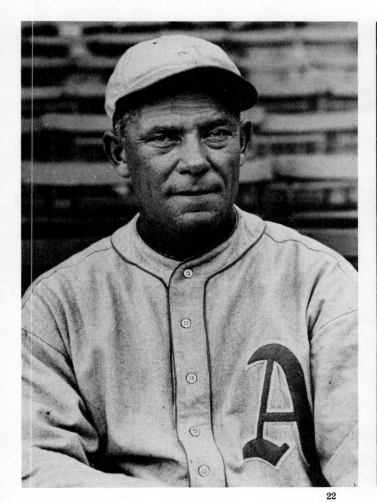

22

23

22. Identify this player, the oldest pitcher to win and to lose a major league game and, even though a pitcher, the oldest player to hit a major league home run in the 20th century.

23. Name this pitcher, the last World War II veteran to play in the major leagues. Early in his career, he pitched the last no-hitter against the New York Yankees. He is one of three pitchers to play for 20 or more years without ever winning 20 games in one year. Name the other two men in this category.

24

25

26

24. This Yankee catcher is remembered today mostly because he became a regular the same day Lou Gehrig took over at first base to begin his 14-year streak of 2130 consecutive games. Identify him.

25. On June 1, 1925, this New York Yankee first baseman got the most famous headache in baseball history; he asked to be excused and was replaced at first base by Gehrig.

26. Name this player, the Yankee who replaced Gehrig at first on May 2, 1939.

27. Gehrig's streak of 2130 consecutive games is an all-time record which has never seriously been challenged. Next to Gehrig, this National Leaguer played more consecutive games at first base than anyone else. Who is he?

28. This pitcher is one of two 20th-century players to lead the league in losses one year and in wins the next, losing more than 20 games the first year and winning more than 20 the second. Name him and the other man who performed this remarkable turnaround.

29. This pitcher is one of four additional pitchers who led the league in losses one year and wins the next; these four, however, didn't both lose and win 20 or more games—they simply led the league in losses and wins in consecutive years. Identify him and name the other three men in this category.

30

30. Who is this pitcher—he was the losing pitcher in the only World Series game ever *won* by the Philadelphia Phillies?

31. This Hall of Famer lost more games in his career than any other man who pitched his whole career in the National League. Name him. Who was the only pitcher in modern baseball history to lead his league in losses in four consecutive years?

31

32

33

32. Name this man, the first major league player to have 3000 hits.

33. This Hall of Famer who played at the turn of the century is remembered for the highest one season batting average ever achieved in the history of major league baseball. Identify him.

34

35

34. This turn-of-the-century player's nickname was "The Tabasco Kid"; a shortstop, he batted .271 in 14 years with three seasons over .300 and had 213 stolen bases. Identify him.

35. Who is this great 19th-century pitcher? He won 198 games and lost 122 in an 11-year career with St. Louis in the American Association and Boston and Cleveland in the National League between 1889 and 1899. In 1891 and 1892 he performed the rare feat of winning more than 30 games in each of two consecutive years.

36

39

36–38. Here are three of the five men who have pitched two no-hitters in the same season. Name them and the other two pitchers who have done this. Including **38** and **39,** five National League pitchers have lost games in which they pitched no-hitters by giving up hits in extra innings. Identify these two and name the other three men in this category.

40. One of the two no-hitters pitched by the pitcher in **36** was the first ever pitched in a night game. The man in **40** pitched the second night-time no-hitter. Identify him. Name the only pitcher to pitch a nine-inning no-hitter, give up a hit in extra innings and continue on to win the game anyway.

38   40

41

41. This player was hired by the man in **44** as baseball's first regular professional coach. He is also the oldest man ever to steal a base in a major league game. Identify him.

42. This Brooklyn Dodger led the National League in stolen bases in 1942 with 20 and in 1946 with 34. A fearless outfielder, injuries suffered while crashing into fences chasing fly balls shortened his career. He was also the youngest National League batting champion. Who is he?

43. This Hall of Famer led his league in stolen bases more times than any other outfielder. Name him. Who was the only player in the 20th century to steal 75 or more bases in a year and *not* lead the major leagues in that department that year? Among all the players in the 20th century who stole more than 75 bases in one year, who had the lowest batting average?

44. As a player, this man stole more bases than any other third baseman in the Hall of Fame. Today he is best remembered as the winner of ten pennants during his 33-year career as a major league manager. Name him and the Hall of Fame third baseman with the *fewest* career stolen bases.

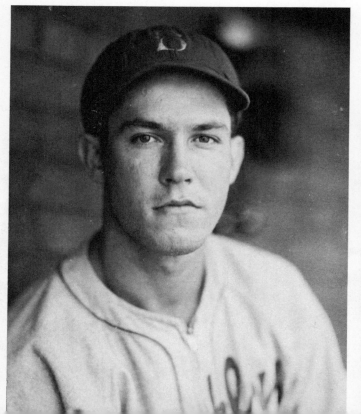

42

43

45

46

45. Identify this great National League hitter. Among the players who hit 50 or more home runs in a year, he struck out and walked the fewest times during his 50 home run year. Which player hit the most triples during a year in which he also hit 50 or more home runs?

46 & 47. These two great National League hitters are two of the seven non-pitchers in major league history who played an entire career of 20 or more seasons with only one team. Name them. Name the other five men in this category. Which of the men pictured was *both* the last player to get 100 or more extra base hits in a year and the player with the most career home runs among those players who *never* led the league in home runs?

48

49

48. Identify this Hall of Fame pitcher from the second and third decades of this century. With which other Hall of Fame pitcher does he share the exact same totals of career wins and career complete games as well as the record for most seasons with more than 25 victories among 20th-century pitchers?

49. Who is this—the only pitcher in this century to win more than 25 games in one season *without* pitching a shutout?

50. This Hall of Famer won 210 games during a 16-year career. He also pitched more innings in World Series competition than any other pitcher from a non-New York team. Name him. Who are the three New York pitchers who pitched more World Series innings?

51 & 52. Six third basemen—three from each league—have been named Most Valuable Player. Name the two third basemen MVPs, one from each league, pictured here, and the other four so honored. Which of the two shown here was also the first unanimous MVP selection? Name the four third basemen who have been named Rookie of the Year.

53. Identify this New York Yankee infielder. In 1953 he set a record for hits in a six-game World Series. Who had the most hits ever in a four-game World Series?

54-56. The three players pictured on these pages are the only three Hall of Fame players who compiled career winning percentages as managers *lower* than their lifetime batting averages. Name them. What man who managed in the major leagues for only one year (but was his team's only manager that year) had the best winning percentage? Can you name the only major league manager born during the 20th century outside the continental United States?

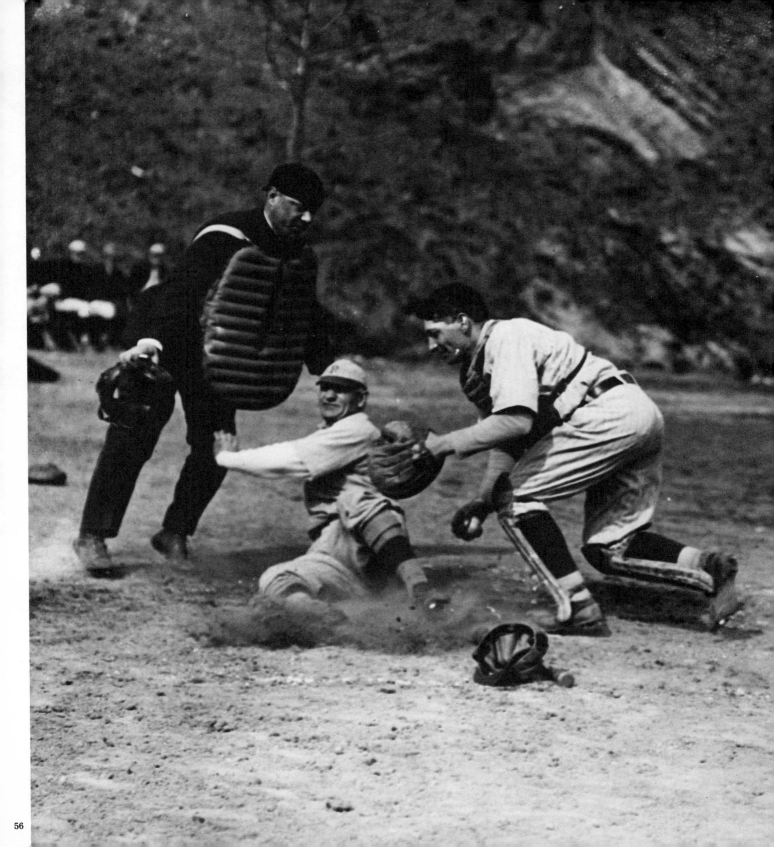

57–59. Here are three of the four pitchers who had careers of 20 years or more entirely with one team. Name them and the other pitcher in this category. Which had the most career wins? Which one was the last pitcher to start 20 or more games in one year and complete them all? Which one of these four men had the most career wins by any modern pitcher who never led his league in wins?

59

60

60. This pitcher is one of only two men to pitch in the major leagues for 22 consecutive calendar years. Who is he and who is the other man to accomplish this?

61

61–64. The pitcher in **61** is one of two winners of three games in a five-game World Series. Who is he? Who is the only other pitcher to accomplish this feat? Six other pitchers have compiled a 3–0 record in a World Series, regardless of the number of games, including the pitchers in **62** and **63**. Identify them and name the other four pitchers in this category. The pitcher in **61** is also one of only three men to win as many as five World Series games during their careers without losing a World Series game. The pitcher in **64** is one of the other men in this group. Identify him. Both **61** and **64** were 5–0 in World Series play; who is the only pitcher with a lifetime 6–0 World Series record? Who pitched the most innings in a single World Series?

63

64

67

65. Identify this third baseman—he was the youngest non-pitcher ever to appear in a World Series. Who was the youngest player ever to hit a home run in the major leagues?

66. The youngest player to hit 100 major league home runs.

67. The youngest player to hit 200 major league home runs. Identify both of these players. The player in **67** also holds the record for most home runs on the road in a single year by a National Leaguer. Who holds the American League record?

68. Who is this teammate of the player in **67**? He led the National League in stolen bases his first three years in the major leagues.

69. This player is one of two left-handed hitting and right-handed throwing athletes to collect more than 3000 hits. Who is he and who is the other player in this category? The player in **69** also had the most career hits by any man who *never* led his league in hits.

70. While the player in **69** held down second, this man was the first baseman on one of baseball's great pre-World War I infields. Who was he? Who were the shortstop and third baseman on that team? The third baseman was the first man to hit World Series home runs on consecutive days.

71. Until recently this Chicago Cub third baseman was credited with having won a triple crown in 1912. A review of the statistics revealed that another man actually led the National League in runs batted in that year. Who is this player and who is the man who was belatedly honored as the 1912 National League RBI leader?

72

73

72 & 73. Here are two of the three men who managed major league teams for 20 or more years and finished as managers with winning percentages under .500. Name them and the third man in this category, the only one of the three who never won a pennant. What manager with over 1000 wins came closest to finishing at exactly .500?

74. This highly recognizable character has the distinction of being the only man to be the minor league Manager-of-the-Year one year and major league Manager-of-the-Year the next. Name him. Who was the only man to be a major league player, manager and umpire?

75

76

75. Identify this pitcher—the first man to win at least one game in four consecutive World Series.

76 & 77. These two pitchers gave up the first and last of Babe Ruth's 60 home runs in 1927. Who are they? Which one of them established a World Series single-game record for strikeouts in 1929 that lasted until 1953? Who broke it? Name the two American League pitchers who share the record for pitching seven shutouts while leading the league in losses. Which one of them is the only pitcher ever to lead the league in losses *and* lowest earned-run average the same year? What National League pitcher had the most shutouts while leading the league in losses?

78 & 79. The player sliding into third base in **78** and the player in **79** are the only players to win just one league batting championship while leading their leagues in stolen bases the same year. The player in **79** also had the lowest career batting average of any player who won just *one* league batting title. Identify him.

80. This man is one of only three players ever to win a batting championship one year yet be traded the next. Who is he? Who are the other batting leaders so traded? What American League player stole the most bases in a year since Ty Cobb stole 96 in 1915? What player who played his whole career with one team had the most career stolen bases?

82

83

81 & 82. These are the only two pitchers to win more than 25 games in a single season during the 1950s. One of them was the first man to win the Most Valuable Player and Cy Young awards the same year. Identify them.

83. This pitcher is one of three to have ten or more shutouts in a single season during the 1960s. Who is he? Who are the other two pitchers to do this? One of the other two, a National Leaguer, holds the major league record for most consecutive pitching appearances as a starter. Who holds the American League record in this department? Who has the most career wins by a pitcher born in a non-English-speaking country outside the Western Hemisphere?

84

85

86

84. This shortstop committed the most errors ever by one man, eight, in a World Series. He was also the youngest manager ever in the major leagues. Identify him.

85. This player is one of two Hall of Fame shortstops who committed six errors in a World Series. Who is he? Who is the other one? The player in **85** played 1103 consecutive games at shortstop. Is this a record for shortstops?

86. Identify this shortstop—the only major leaguer who has had an expressway in a major city named after him.

87. Name this shortstop—he had the highest single-season batting average of any modern National League shortstop. Who had the highest single-season batting average among modern American League shortstops?

88. This pitcher had the highest career batting average of any pitcher with at least 500 times at bat in the major leagues. He is also the only pitcher to win *exactly* 200 games during his career. Name him. Name the pitcher with the highest batting average among those pitchers with over 300 career times at bat.

89. Identify the only pitcher ever to hit two triples in a World Series game.

90. This pitcher is one of only two men to pitch 20 or more seasons in the major leagues and never hit a home run. Who is he? Who is the other pitcher in this category? Who is the only pitcher to hit a grand slam home run in a World Series game?

91. Here is the first pitcher to hit a home run in the World Series. Who is this American Leaguer? Who was the first National League pitcher to hit a World Series home run?

51

93

92 & 93. There were no regular season perfect games pitched in the major leagues during the 42 years between the masterpiece pitched in 1922 by the pitcher in **92** and the one pitched in 1964 by the pitcher in **93**. Who were these two perfect game pitchers?

94

94. Name this pitcher—he had the best single-season winning percentage of any American League pitcher with at least 15 decisions. Who holds the National League record in this department?

95. This man was the first black pitcher in the National League. Identify him. What major league pitcher retired the most consecutive batters? Only two 300-game career winners have ever led the league in losses. Who were they?

96

97

99

96–100. Identify these five figures: the centerfielder, first baseman, third baseman, shortstop and manager of the infamous 1919 Chicago "Black Sox." These four players, and four others, were banned from baseball for life following the 1920 season, a full year after they lost the fixed World Series to the Cincinnati Reds. Which one of those pictured set a major league record in that year for hits in a single season by a switch-hitter?

100

102

101 & 102. Identify the first baseman in **101**—the only left-handed throwing, right-handed batting player ever to win a batting championship. He and the player in **102** are two of the three men who received votes in the inaugural Hall of Fame balloting in 1936 who have not yet been elected to the Hall. Who is the third man in this group? Who was the last left-throwing and right-batting non-pitcher to hit .300 in the major leagues?

101

103

103. This player made his name in college football and track. During a six-year major league baseball career his statistics were not remarkable, but he did drive in the only run scored in baseball's only nine-inning double no-hitter. Who is he? Who were the winning and losing pitchers in that game? Who was the only Heisman Trophy winner to play in the major leagues?

104. One of the first black players in the major leagues, this third baseman's seven bases on balls in the 1954 World Series set a record for a four-game Series. Who is he?

105

106

105. Identify this Yankee pitcher whose brief career saw him on some of the Yankees' strongest teams. He was the winning pitcher in the final games of two World Series swept in four straight by the Yankees.

106. This Yankee outfielder was a lifetime .325 hitter and hit .350 in 16 World Series games. He led the American League in hits with 231 in 1927, the same year Babe Ruth hit 60 home runs. Who is he? What Yankee pitcher was the only Rookie-of-the-Year to win 20 games?

107. Name this Yankee pitcher who scored the first run and won the first game ever played at Yankee Stadium.

109

108. This great Detroit hitter led the American League in batting in four odd-numbered years during the 1920s, including 1927, the year Ruth connected for 60 home runs. Who is he?

109. This Yankee leftfielder had a good year himself in 1927—a .337 average with eight home runs and 103 runs batted in. He is the only American League player to "hit for the cycle"—a single, double, triple and home run in one game—three times during his career. Identify him. Who is the only National Leaguer to do this?

108

110

111

110. Ruth and Gehrig were first and second in bases on balls in the American League in 1927 with 138 and 109 respectively. This Philadelphia Athletics second baseman was third with 105. He also set a record for second basemen with 53 consecutive errorless games in 1932. Who is he? Who broke this record?

111. This Philadelphia Phillie shared the National League lead in home runs in 1927 with 30, half of Ruth's total. Who is he? What other National Leaguer hit 30 home runs that year?

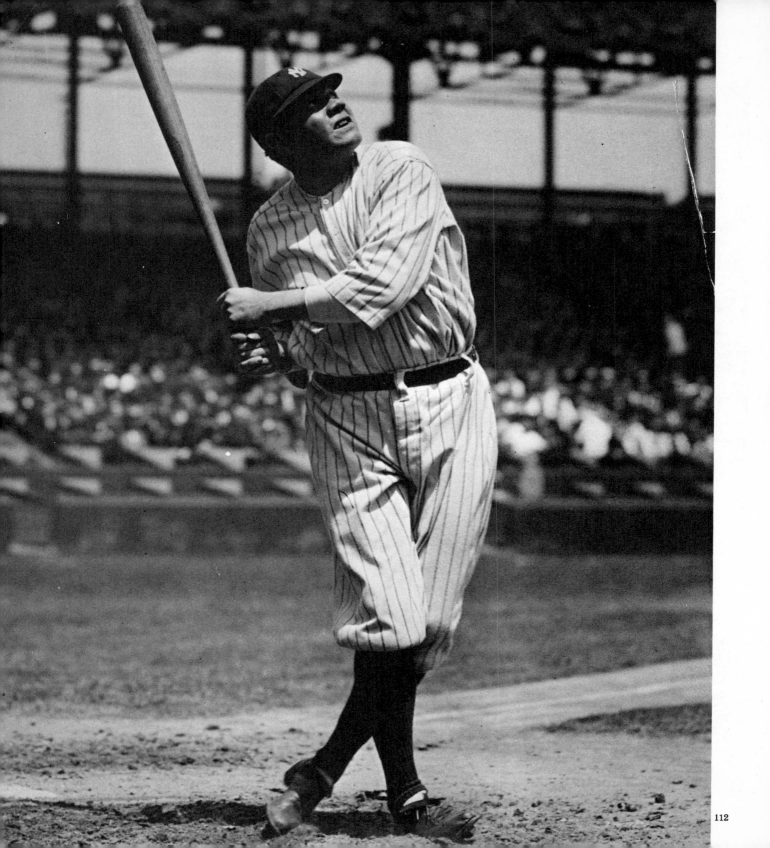

113

114

112-114. Identify the player pictured here, the only man thrown out stealing to end a World Series. Another one of these three players was the winning pitcher in that crucial Series game. Name him. The man thrown out stealing and the third man pictured here hit the only two home runs in the first All Star game. Identify the third man. Which one of these two players scored more runs in a single season than any other player in the 20th century? He is also one of three men to have a 200-hit season which included 50 home runs. Who are the other two? What player had the most pinch hits in a single season during the 1920s?

115

116

117

118

115. This early 20th-century pitcher is the only pitcher to bat for himself as the last man retired in a nine-inning perfect game in this century. Who is he? Who pitched that perfect game? This man also registered more than 200 strikeouts during each of six seasons. Is this a major league record?

116 & 117. These two New York Giant pitchers were teammates on two pennant-winning teams in the 1930s. One of them set a record by shutting out Cincinnati in four consecutive starting appearances against the Reds in the same year. No other pitcher has shut out one team in more consecutive starts against that team. Which one of these two did this?

118. This Giant of a later era is the only Japanese native to pitch in the major leagues. Name him.

120

119-121. The three pitchers pictured on these pages are three of the nine pitchers in the 20th century to lead the league in wins one year and in losses the next. One of these three was the only Cy Young Award winner to pitch on a last-place team. Another is the only pitcher ever to win consecutive Most Valuable Player awards. Identify these three and name the other six men who have led the league in wins one year and losses the next. What pitcher gave up the fewest hits in two consecutive World Series complete game victories?

122

122. Name this one-armed outfielder who played with the St. Louis Browns during 1945.

123. This man, who played during World War II, was the only player certifiably blind in one eye to pitch in the major leagues. Identify him.

124. Who is this pitcher, the first major league ballplayer to be drafted in World War II?

125. Right after the war, this player set a record which has never been equalled; he became the only man ever to lead the league both in *most* home runs and *fewest* strikeouts for the season among regular players. Name him.

123

124

125

127

126 & 127. The only brothers to hit back-to-back home runs in the major leagues. They are also the only brothers victimized in the same unassisted triple play. Identify them. Who executed the only unassisted triple play in a night game?

128

129

128 & 129. These two men are the only two brothers to pitch against each other in a National League game. Who are they? When did two brothers lead the American and National Leagues in wins and games started in the same year?

130

130 & 131. Identify these two players, both Hall of Famers, who are the only winners of two triple crowns. One of them had the highest lifetime batting average of any player who played his whole career with one team. The other player pictured here is the only non-outfielder and non-first baseman ever to collect 240 or more hits in a year. He is also the only player ever to lead the league in home runs in a year in which he got more than 240 hits. What American League player hit the most home runs in his home stadium in one season? Of all the players who played 20 years or more in the major leagues, which had the highest career World Series batting average?

72

133

132 & 133. Identify the two players who share the highest batting average for a player with more than 240 hits in a year. They are also the only two players to lead the league in stolen bases in years in which they had more than 240 hits. One of them had the most stolen bases and the fewest home runs of any player to win a triple crown; he became, in his triple crown year, the only player ever to steal more than 75 bases while leading the league in home runs. The other is the only Hall of Famer ever to have two sons who played in the major leagues. Name them.

134. This player had the lowest batting average, but also the fewest strikeouts, of any player with more than 240 hits in a year. Identify him.

135. This first baseman batted .273 for 16 years, 1907–26, with four teams, but is primarily remembered for having committed a catastrophic base-running mistake that cost the Giants the 1908 pennant.

136. These two infielders are two of the Chicago Cubs' three all-time leaders in stolen bases. They are, in fact, the Hall of Fame's leading shortstop and second baseman in stolen bases among players who *never* led the league in that category and played their whole careers in the 20th century. Identify them. Who is the Cub's all-time stolen-base leader? Name the second baseman who is the only player in major league history to have two separate streaks of more than 500 consecutive games played.

137. This player is one of three Washington Senators to lead the American League in runs batted in. Who is he? Who were the other two?

138. This Washington Senator leads all third basemen in consecutive games played. He also walked more than any other player in one year during the 1950s. His ability to draw bases on balls—he led the league in walks six times—earned him the nickname "The Walking Man." Who is he? Who had the most bases on balls in one year in the 1960s?

139. This player played more than half of his 20-year career (1939–60) for Washington. He played more games at first base, 2237, than any other American Leaguer in history. Who is he? Name the player who spent 19 of his 20 major league seasons with the Senators and struck out fewer times than any other 20-year player.

140. This player spent 18 of his 20 major league seasons, 1915–34, at first base for the Senators. He batted over .300 ten times for Washington, and led or tied for the league lead in fielding six times. Name him.

140

142

141-143. Here are three of the six players to hit 25 or more triples in one year in the 20th century. The player in **141** had the highest lifetime batting average among players who *never* led the league in batting, while another one of those pictured here is the only infielder among the six. Name the three players pictured here and the other three players with 25 or more triples in one year. Who was the only player to hit four triples in a single World Series?

145

146

144. The man pictured here is one of three pitchers in the 20th century who won 20 or more games in their *final* season in the major leagues. Who is he? Who were the other two? One of the other two is the only man to pitch one no-hitter in each of four consecutive years.

145. Name the winning pitcher in the most one-sided All Star game.

146. Who is the only Rookie-of-the-Year pitcher who did not have a winning percentage over .500. What Hall of Fame pitcher was the oldest when he won his first major league game? Who is the only pitcher to pitch more than 3000 major league innings without giving up a grand slam home run?

148

149

147–149. Name these three hitting stars of the 1930s. Two of them are the only players ever to have 240 or more hits in a year and not lead their league in hits, while the third is the man who got the most bases on balls, but also the fewest stolen bases of any player with 240 or more hits in a year. Who was the only 19th-century player to have 240 or more hits in a year? Who had the fewest home runs among non-pitchers who played an entire career of 20 seasons or more all in the 20th century?

150

151

152

150–152. Only 15 times in baseball history has a player driven in 165 or more runs in a single year, yet this feat was accomplished by four players in 1930. Three of these four are pictured on these pages. Name them and the fourth man in this group. One of these, in another year, got the most hits ever in a year by a right-handed batter. Another holds the all-time record for runs batted in a single year. The third, the only American Leaguer, has the highest all-time runs batted in total among players who played their entire career with one team. He is also the only man to hit four home runs in a four-game World Series. Who was the only 19th-century player to drive in 165 or more runs in a single year? Who was the only player to hit home runs in three consecutive All Star games?

154

155

156

153. It should be easy to identify this National League pitcher who dominated the scene in the mid-1930s. Who hit the line drive in the 1937 All Star game that broke his toe, eventually bringing his great career to an end?

154. Name this pitcher—the only man to lose two World Series games on consecutive days and, in another year, win two World Series games on consecutive days.

155. This man is the only pitcher ever to lose an All Star and a World Series game in the same year for two consecutive years. Identify him.

156. This pitcher is one of six men to win an All Star and World Series game the same year, doing it in 1940. Name him. Who were the other five who did this? What 300-game-winning pitcher was the oldest when he won his first game in the major leagues?

157

158

157. This man is the last player to lead the league in hitting while playing for an eighth-place team. Identify him.

158. This one-time winner of a league batting championship won the crown with the largest percentage differential between his *career* batting average and his league-leading *season's* average. Name him.

159

159. This man had the highest American League batting average ever—and, in the same year, won the batting title by the biggest percentage margin ever. Who is he?

160. This player—and the player in **159**—are the only two men to lead the league in fielding during a year in which they won triple crowns. Identify him. Who is the only batting champion whose career batting average was higher than his average during the season he led the league?

163

161 & 162. These two players are the only two ever to hit 50 or more home runs in a year and *not* lead the league in home runs, as well as the only two ever to win a league batting championship in a year in which they hit 50 or more home runs. One is the player with the most career home runs among players who played their whole career with one team, while the other is the only man to hit 50 or more home runs in different years for two different franchises.

163. Identify this player—the only one ever to hit home runs in his first two major league times at bat. One of the three players pictured has by far the most career home runs by a switch-hitter. Who is second in this category? Who is the only player ever to hit a grand-slam home run in the seventh game of a World Series?

164. Identify this National Leaguer who holds the major league record for most pinch-hit home runs in a year.

165. This player holds the American League record for most pinch-hit home runs in a year. He also holds the major league record for having at least one run batted in in 12 consecutive games. Who is he?

166. One of the great pinch hitters of all time, this man is remembered today for his exploits with the Giants in the 1954 World Series when he victimized Cleveland pitching for seven RBIs in only six at bats. Identify him.

167. An outfielder and outstanding pinch hitter for 20 major league seasons, in 1949 this man became the only American League player ever to hit three bases-loaded triples in one game. Who is he? Who was the first player to get 20 pinch hits in one season? Who was the only player to get 20 pinch hits in a season twice?

168. In 1932 this player set a record which still stands; he got nine hits in an 18-inning game, the most hits ever by a player in one game regardless of the length of the game. Identify him.

164

167

166

168

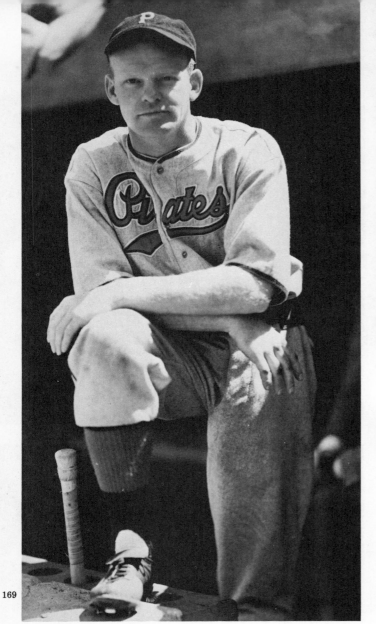

169

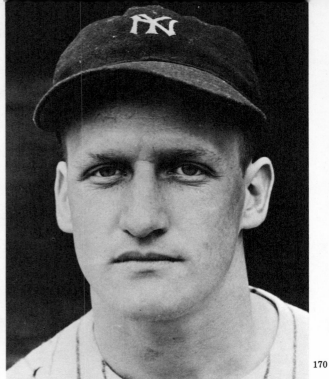

170

169. Identify this National League pitcher who had a 143–97 record over 13 seasons (1932–49), but is best remembered for giving up a famous home run in the 1946 All Star Game.

170. This 1940s right-hander helped both the Yankees and the Cubs win pennants in the 1940s and is the only pitcher to win 20 games in one year pitching in both leagues. Who is he?

171. This 5′6″ left-hander was the American League's Most Valuable Player in 1952 when he won 24 and lost seven for the Philadelphia Athletics. He later led the American League in earned run average while helping the Yankees to a pennant. Identify him.

172

173

172. Identify this relief pitcher who never pitched a complete game in the major leagues, yet three times led the National League in appearances by a pitcher, and twice led the American League in saves.

173. An early relief specialist, this pitcher led the American League in games pitched in six times during his 14-year career (1923–36). Who is he?

174

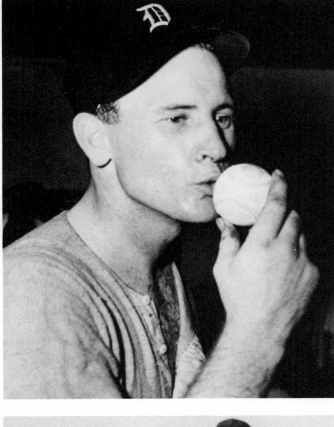

175

177

176

174. Playing in both leagues, this pitcher won 158 games and lost 101 over 15 seasons between 1933 and 1949. In 1934 with Detroit he tied the American League record for consecutive wins in a season. Who is he?

175. Identify this player, one of two Detroit pitchers to lead the American League in earned run average during the 1940s. He had a great year in 1944—27–14, 2.12 ERA, 33 complete games and seven shutouts. Who was the other Tiger pitcher to lead to league in ERA during the 1940s?

176. This National Leaguer is one of only four pitchers since 1900 to pitch consecutive one-hitters. His overall record for 15 seasons between 1930 and 1945 was 193–121, including three seasons with 20 wins or more. Identify him.

177. An era in baseball history ended when this great Hall of Famer retired after the 1934 season. Identify him and explain why. Name the left-hander who had the lowest ERA in a year in which he pitched 300 or more innings. What 19th-century pitcher won the most one-sided no-hitter in history?

178

179

180

178. Name this player—the only non-Yankee to hit ten or more World Series home runs.

179. This Dodger outfielder was one of four players ever to hit the famous "Hit Sign Win Suit" sign in Ebbets Field and collect a suit from Brooklyn tailor Abe Stark; he is the only man to do this twice. Name him.

180. Name this prominent Dodger pitcher of the 1930s. In 1934 he beat the Giants on the next-to-last day of the season, enabling St. Louis to win the pennant. He has one of the most memorable names in baseball history. Who was the first National Leaguer to hit a grand-slam home run in World Series play?

181. In 1953 this Dodger catcher set a record for home runs by a catcher in one year which stood until 1970. Who is he? Who broke the record? The catcher in 181 also stole fewer bases than any other catcher in the Hall of Fame except one. Who?

182

183

184

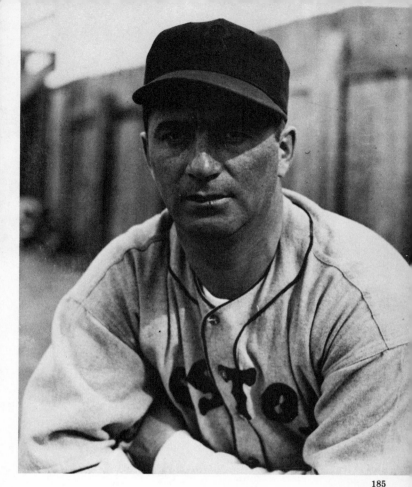

185

182. Who is this player, the first major leaguer to enlist in World War I? His .545 batting average in the 1914 World Series was the best in a four-game Series until it was surpassed in 1928. By whom?

183. This Dodger pitcher threw a one-hit, 6–0 shutout in his final game in 1942, a game in which he faced the minimum 27 batters. After that game, he entered the U.S. Navy where he remained for 27 years, making this the most impressive career finale ever pitched. Who was he?

184. This Dodger catcher hit the first pinch-hit home run in an All Star game. Identify him.

185. This catcher played in the major leagues for several teams between 1923 and 1939. He is remembered today for his activities as a counter-intelligence officer during World War II. Who was he? What non-pitcher had the lowest career batting average among players who spent at least 15 seasons in the major leagues?

186

187

186. The last playing manager to win a World Series, this shortstop stole fewer bases during his career than any other American League shortstop in the Hall of Fame. Identify him. What National League Hall of Fame shortstop stole fewer bases than this man?

187. Identify the only man to be both a Rookie-of-the-Year and a Manager-of-the-Year. Name the other two Rookies-of-the-Year to become major league managers.

188. Name this man, one of three to appear both in a World Series and a Rose Bowl. Who are the other two? Who was the manager of the only team in baseball history to win two consecutive pennants with the same won-and-lost record each year? Which National and American League managers won pennants by the biggest margins?

189. During the decade of the 1920s the Yankees played 1535 regular season games. This man was their manager for 1524 of those games. Who is he? Who managed the other 11 games?

188

192

190. This St. Louis Cardinal is one of two players to bat .500 in a seven-game World Series. Who is he? Who else did it?

191. Though shown here in a Dodger uniform, this player is best remembered as a colorful member of the St. Louis Cardinals, for whom he had a remarkable 20 pinch hits in 43 appearances as a pinch-hitter in 1938. Identify him.

192. This Yankee had the most stolen bases of any player in one year during the 1930s. Who is he?

193. This man has an unusual claim to fame—he is the only major leaguer whose last name is the same as the name of the town in which he was born. Who is he?

195

196

194–196. The players in **194** and **195** hold the National and American League records for home runs in a calendar month. Name them. The players in **194** and **196** had the most and the least stolen bases of any player with 50 or more home runs in a year. Identify the player in **196**. He also had the lowest batting average of any player with 50 or more home runs in a year. What Yankee had the most home runs in the World Series of 1961, the year the team as a whole hit 240 homers during the season? Who was the first player to hit two World Series home runs in one game?

198

197. Identify this Hall of Fame National League shortstop, one of the few players in major league history to play for 23 seasons.

198. Identify this man who stole fewer bases in his career than any other second baseman in the Hall of Fame.

200

199. Remembered as one of the great fielding outfielders of the 1950s, this player accomplished the rare feat of getting six hits in six times at bat on June 10, 1953. Name him. What outfielder had the most assists in a single season in the 20th century?

200. Who is this player who batted .300 or more ten times, and ended a 19-year career in 1959 as a lifetime .300 hitter. He is best remembered today for scoring the winning run in the seventh game of the 1946 World Series, running all the way from first on a single to give the Cardinals a 4–3 Series win over the Red Sox. Who hit that single? Name the two St. Louis Cardinals who were the only players during the 1950s to have 20 pinch hits in a season. Who is the only player ever to steal 75 or more bases in a year in which he failed to hit a home run? Who is the only player to steal seven bases in a seven-game World Series?

201

202

203

201. This player is one of two pitchers who won 200 major league games, but lost more than they won. Who is he? Who is the other pitcher in this category?

202. Identify this player—he had the fewest career hits of any non-pitcher who played 20 years or more in the major leagues.

203. It should be easy to identify this pitcher—he was the first 30-game winner since Dizzy Dean in 1934. What 300-game winner was youngest when he scored his first major league victory?

204. Name this National League pitcher of the 1950s and early 1960s. In 1969 he entered Congress as a Republican representative from North Carolina. Name the three pitchers who led the league in losses and strikeouts the same year. Who were the only father and son pitchers in major league history who both led the league in losses one year?

20

205

206

205. In 1935, two playing managers opposed each other in the World Series for the last time. This man was one of them. Who was he? Who was the other?

206. This man had the highest single-season batting average ever for a catcher. Name him.

207. This man is the only catcher ever to win two league batting championships. Who is he?

208. This man shares with another the National League record for most years with 100 or more games played as a catcher. Name him and the co-holder.

209

209. Identify this catcher, who holds the record for most years leading the league in putouts by a catcher.

210. This Philadelphia Athletic catcher set a record in 1946 when he handled 605 chances flawlessly in 117 games for a fielding average of 1.000—something no other catcher has ever done. Name him.

210

211

211. Identify this player, the only major leaguer to get three hits in one inning.

212. Who is this player, the first after World War II to hit four home runs in a game?

212

213

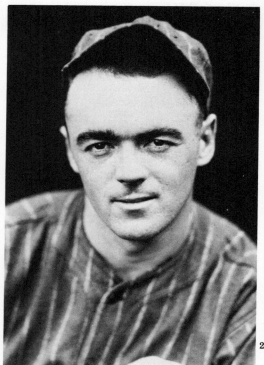

214

215

216

213. Identify this second baseman who was a .303 lifetime hitter over 17 seasons with the Senators and Red Sox (1925–41). He led the American League in batting with a .349 average in 1935.

214. This White Sox third baseman led American League third basemen in fielding for six years in a row during the 1920s. Name him.

215. Who is this second baseman who played most of his career with the White Sox and set a major league record by having the fewest strikeouts in the league for 12 years in a row?

216. This is one major leaguer it should be possible to identify from the shape of his bat alone. Name him.

218

219

217. Who is this Baltimore first baseman who tied the American League record with 11 runs batted in one game on July 6, 1966?

218. Who is this man, the first Hall of Famer born outside the continental United States?

219. The first black player in the American League, this man made his debut on July 3, 1947. He went on to lead the American League in home runs twice and runs batted in twice. Identify him.

220. This National Leaguer had the lowest career batting average of any player with 1000 or more career extra-base hits. Identify him. What triple crown winner had the lowest average in the year he won the triple crown? Who holds the record for being hit by pitches the most times in one year? Whose record did he break?

220

ANSWERS

1 & 2. Harry Walker, **1,** and Dixie Walker, **2,** were the only brothers to win a league batting championship each. Harry led the National League with .363 average in 1947 while dividing the year between St. Louis and Philadelphia. Dixie won the National League batting title with a .357 average in 1944 with the Brooklyn Dodgers. **3 & 4.** Vince DiMaggio, **3,** and Joe DiMaggio, **4,** each hit a home run in All Star games. Joe hit his in 1939 at New York as the American League won, 3–1. Vince, then with the Pirates, connected in the 1943 game at Philadelphia, also won by the American League, 5–3. Eddie and Johnny O'Brien, born December 11, 1930, were the most recent set of twin brothers to play in the major leagues. Eddie played five years for Pittsburgh, 1953–58, batting .236 in 231 games, mostly as a shortstop and outfielder. Johnny O'Brien played six years, 1953–59, for Pittsburgh, St. Louis and Milwaukee. He compiled a .250 average in 339 games, mostly as a second baseman.

5 & 6. Dale Alexander, **5,** and Bill Terry, **6.** Alexander led the American League in batting in 1932 with a .367 average while dividing the year between Detroit and Boston. His major league career only spanned five years, 1929–33, the shortest of any player to win a league batting championship. Terry's .401 average with the 1930 New York Giants was the highest leading average among the 20th-century players who won only one batting title. **7 & 8.** Tris Speaker, **7,** and Phil Cavaretta, **8.** Speaker led the American League with a .386 average at Cleveland in 1916. Cavaretta took the National League title with a .355 average playing for the 1945 Cubs. In addition to Speaker and Cavaretta, the following four 20-year players won just one batting crown during their long careers: Babe Ruth (.378 with the 1924 Yankees); Willie Mays (.345 with the 1954 Giants); Al Kaline (.340 with the 1955 Tigers); Frank Robinson (.316 with the 1966 Orioles).

9–11. The three Dodger managers pictured are: **9,** Leo Durocher, shown during his playing years as a shortstop. He managed the Dodgers from 1939 through 1946, and for the first half of 1948. **10,** Charlie Dressen, Dodger manager from 1951 through 1953; **11,** Walter Alston, Dodger manager from 1954 through 1976. The other two Dodger managers were Burt Shotton, 1947 and the last half of 1948 through 1950, and Tom LaSorda, 1977–present. (LaSorda actually took over from Alston with four games remaining in 1976.) Alston, shown here as a young ballplayer, came up to bat once with the Cardinals in 1936, and was struck out by Lon Warnecke. His 23 years managing the Dodgers are surpassed only by Connie Mack's 50 years with the Philadelphia Athletics (1901–50) and John McGraw's 30 years with the New York Giants (1902–32). **12.** Don Drysdale; he pitched 14 years for Alston, 1956–69.

13. Vada Pinson. Billy Williams of the Chicago Cubs set the record for consecutive games played by a National League outfielder with 1117 between 1963 and 1970, the third-longest consecutive-game streak in history. Willie Mays' 660 home runs puts him third on the all-time list, the most by a man who never led the league in runs batted in. Mays' 1903 RBIs puts him seventh all-time in that category, but the league leadership always eluded him; his best year was 1962 when he drove in 141, the year Tommy Davis of the Dodgers had 153. **14.** Hank Aaron. His 6856 total bases heads the all-time list, with Stan Musial second at 6134 and Willie Mays third with 6066. They are the only three players to go over the 6000 total base mark. Musial easily had the highest career average of the three, .331, compared to Aaron's .305 and Mays' .302. **15.** Willie Stargell. He hit three home runs in a game twice in 1971. The other National Leaguers to do this are Johnny Mize, Ralph Kiner and Willie Mays—in one of these games Mays hit four home runs. The only American Leaguer to hit three home runs in a game twice in one year is Ted Williams, 1957.

16. Eddie Plank, winner of 327 games during his 17-year career (1901–17) with the Philadelphia Athletics and St. Louis teams in the Federal and American Leagues. Warren Spahn is the only left-hander in major league history who won more games—363 for the Braves, Mets and Giants between 1942 and 1965. **17.** Ray Chapman, Cleveland shortstop, was killed by a pitch thrown by Carl Mays, then with the Yankees, at New York on August 16, 1920. **18.** Carl Mays, who pitched and won his two complete games for the Red Sox against the Athletics on August 30, 1918, by scores of 12–0 and 4–1. He was with the Giants in 1929 when this picture was taken. **19.** William Leopold (Spittin' Bill) Doak, one of the last legal spitballers in the major leagues. He pitched and won two complete games for the Cardinals against the Dodgers on September 18, 1917. The scores were 2–0 and 12–4. The last pitcher to do this was Dutch Levsen of the Cleveland Indians, who beat the Red Sox twice on August 28, 1926, 6–1 and 5–1.

20. Nick Altrock. A final base hit in 1929 made him also the oldest man to get a hit in the major leagues until Minnie Minoso singled in a special appearance with the White Sox in September, 1976. Minoso was 53, about nine months older than Altrock when he got his last hit. **21.** Satchel Paige, who became the first black pitcher in the American League when he joined the Cleveland Indians in 1948. Paige left the American League in 1953 but came out of retirement in 1965 to pitch three innings for Kansas City, surrendering no runs and only one hit, to Carl Yastrzemski, at which time he became, at 59, the oldest player ever to appear in a major league game. **22.** Jack Quinn. Quinn pitched for many teams during his 23-year career, compiling a 247–216 record. He became the oldest man to win a major league game with a relief win for Brooklyn on August 14, 1932, just one month after his 48th birthday. Quinn was still 48 when he became the oldest man to lose a major league game during his final season, with Cincinnati, on June 28, 1933. On June 27, 1930, at 45, Quinn became the oldest player to hit a home run in the major leagues in the 20th century. (The oldest player ever to hit a home run was the great Chicago first baseman, Cap Anson—Anson was 46 and at the end of his career in 1897 when he hit his last homer.) **23.** Hoyt Wilhelm, released by the Dodgers in 1972 just before turning 49. On September 2, 1958, Wilhelm pitched the last no-hitter against the Yankees, beating them for Baltimore 1-0. Wilhelm pitched 21 years (1952-72) for many teams, never winning 20 games. His best record was 15-3 in his rookie year with the New York Giants, a win total he matched with a 15-11 year at Baltimore in 1959. The only other two players to pitch 20 or more years without winning 20 games are Lindy McDaniel and Curt Simmons. McDaniel pitched 21 years (1955-75) for several teams. His top year for wins was 1957 when he was 15-9 for the Cardinals. Curt Simmons pitched 20 years (1947-67) for four teams; his top year was 1964, 18-9 with the Cardinals.

24. Benny Bengough. **25.** Wally Pipp. After being replaced by Gehrig, Pipp moved to Cincinnati in 1926, where he finished his career. Pipp should be remembered for more than just being the man who played first for the Yankees, before Gehrig. He batted over .300 three times and led the American League in home runs twice in the dead-ball era with 12 in 1916 and nine in 1917. **26.** Babe Dahlgren. Dahlgren batted .235 with 89 RBIs in 1939, but 1940 was his last year with the Yankees. He was with Boston when this picture was taken. **27.** Gus Suhr, who played in the major leagues for 11 years (1930-40), mostly for Pittsburgh. His 822 consecutive games are the most by a first baseman other than Lou Gehrig.

28. Eddie Rommel. With the Philadelphia Athletics, Rommel led the American League in losses with a 16-23 year in 1921 and came back in 1922 to post a 27-13 record and lead the league in wins. The only pitcher to duplicate this feat was Dolf Luque of Cincinnati, who led the National League in losses with a 13-23 record in 1922, and came back the next year to lead the league in wins with a 27-8 season. **29.** Charlie Root, one of the four additional pitchers to lead the league in losses one year and wins the next. With the Cubs, Root led the National League in losses in 1926 with an 18-17 season, and in wins in 1927 with a 26-15 mark. The other three men in this group are: Hal Newhouser of Detroit, 17-17 in 1947, 21-12 in 1948; Ed Cicotte of the Chicago White Sox, 12-19 in 1918, 29-7 in 1919; Mickey Lolich of Detroit, 14-19 in 1970, 25-14 in 1971. **30.** Ernie Shore. Pitching for Boston, Shore lost the first game of the 1915 World Series to the Phillies and Grover Cleveland Alexander. The Phillies lost the next four games in 1915—Shore won one of them—and four straight in 1950. **31.** Eppa Rixey. Rixey's 251 losses (he won 266 games) are the fifth-highest all-time total, and the most by any pitcher who played his entire career in the National League. Rixey pitched for the Phillies, 1912-20, and the Cincinnati Reds, 1921-33. Pedro Ramos is the only pitcher in modern baseball history to lead the league in losses in four consecutive years. He did this in

1958-61 with the Washington Senators and, after the franchise moved, the Minnesota Twins.

32. Adrian Constantine (Cap) Anson. He collected 3041 hits during his 22 years (1876-97) with the National League Chicago White Stockings. **33.** Hugh Duffy. His .438 batting average with the Boston National League team in 1894 is the best ever recorded. **34.** Norman (Kid) Elberfeld. **35.** John (Happy Jack) Stivetts.

36. Johnny Vander Meer. He pitched the only two no-hitters in consecutive starts on June 11 and June 15, 1938, for Cincinnati against Boston and Brooklyn, winning 3-0 and 6-0. **37.** Virgil Trucks. His two no-hitters came on May 15 and August 25, 1952, for Detroit against Washington and New York. He won both 1-0. **38.** Jim Maloney pitched his two no-hitters for Cincinnati on June 14 and August 9, 1965, against the Mets and Cubs. He beat the Cubs 1-0, but lost in ten innings to the Mets, also 1-0. The other two pitchers to pitch two no-hitters in one year are: Allie Reynolds for the Yankees, who beat Cleveland 1-0 on July 12, 1951, and Boston 8-0 on September 28; Nolan Ryan for the California Angels, who beat Kansas City 3-0 on May 15, 1973, and Detroit 6-0 on July 15. Maloney is the only pitcher to win and lose games in which he pitched no-hitters in the same year. **39.** Leon (Red) Ames, one of the other four National League pitchers, besides Maloney, to lose a game in which he pitched a nine-inning no-hitter. Pitching for the Giants against Brooklyn on opening day, April 15, 1909, Ames gave up a hit in the tenth and lost the game 3-0 in the 13th. The other three National League pitchers to lose games in which they had pitched nine-inning no-hitters are: Jim Vaughan—pitching for the Cubs against Cincinnati on May 2, 1917, Vaughan gave up a hit and lost 1-0 in the tenth; Harry McIntyre—pitching for Brooklyn against Pittsburgh on August 1, 1906, McIntyre gave up a hit in the 11th and lost 1-0 in the 13th; Harvey Haddix—pitching for Pittsburgh against Milwaukee on May 26, 1959, Haddix gave up a hit and lost the game in the 13th after retiring the first 36 batters. **40.** Ewell Blackwell pitched the second night game no-hitter. He beat Boston for Cincinnati, 6-0, on June 18, 1947. Bob Wicker, pitching for Chicago against the New York Giants on June 11, 1904, pitched a nine-inning no-hitter, gave up a hit in the tenth, continued in the game and won 1-0 in 12 innings.

41. Arlie Latham, hired by McGraw to coach the New York Giants in 1909. Latham, who had last played as a regular with the 1895 Cincinnati Reds, made a late-season appearance in 1909 and stole a base, becoming, at 50, the oldest man ever to steal a base in the major leagues. **42.** Pete Reiser. After leaving the Dodgers in 1948, Reiser finished his career with brief stops with the Braves, Pirates and Indians. Reiser was 22 when he won the 1941 National League batting title with a .343 average. **43.** Max Carey led the National League in stolen bases a record 10 times while playing with Pittsburgh from 1910 through 1925. Bob Bescher stole 80 bases for Cincinnati in 1911, leading the National League, but not the majors, led by Ty Cobb's 83 stolen bases. Los Angeles' Davey Lopes stole a league-leading 77 bases in 1975 with a .262 batting average, lowest among those who stole more than 75 in one season. **44.** John McGraw. As a player for 16 years (1891-1906) with several teams, McGraw stole 436 bases. The low total for a Hall of Fame third baseman is the 68 stolen by recently elected Eddie Mathews during 17 seasons (1952–68).

45. John Mize. In 1947, Mize hit 51 home runs for the New York Giants while striking out only 42 times and walking 74 times, the lowest totals recorded in those departments by a player hitting 50 or more home runs in a year. Babe Ruth hit 16 triples to go with his 59 home runs in 1921, a record number for a player with 50 or more home runs in a season. **46.** Mel Ott. **47.** Stan Musial. Ott played 22 years with the New York Giants, 1926–47. Musial played 22 years with the St. Louis Cardinals, 1941–63. The other five non-pitchers who played an entire career of 20 or more seasons with only one team are: Cap Anson, 22 years (1876–97) with the Chicago White Stockings; Luke Appling, 20 years (1930–50) Chicago White Sox; Al Kaline, 22 years (1953–74), Detroit Tigers; Brooks Robinson, 23 years (1955–77), Baltimore Orioles; Carl Yastrzemski, 20 years (1961–80), Boston Red Sox. Musial is both the last player to have 100 or more extra base hits in a year (103 in 1948) and the player with the most career home runs, 475, who never led the league in home runs.

48. Grover Cleveland Alexander. Pitching 20 years (1911–30) for the Phillies, Cubs and Cardinals, Alexander won 373 games and pitched 439 complete games. In 17 years with the Giants (and 1 game for the Reds) from 1900 through 1916, Christy Mathewson also won 373 games and pitched 439 complete games. Alexander and Mathewson each had six seasons with over 25 wins. (Alexander's were 28 in 1911, 27 in 1914, 31 in 1915, 33 in 1916, 30 in 1917, and 27 in 1920; Mathewson's were 30 in 1903, 33 in 1904, 31 in 1905, 37 in 1908, 27 in 1910, and 26 in 1911. **49.** Joe Bush, 26–7 for the 1922 Yankees without a shutout. **50.** Chief Bender. With the Philadelphia Athletics, Bender pitched 85 innings in five World Series—1905, 1910, 1911, 1913, and 1914. The three New York pitchers who top Bender on the all-time World Series innings-pitched list are Whitey Ford (Yankees)—146; Mathewson (Giants)—101.2; Red Ruffing (Yankees)—85.2.

51. Al Rosen (Cleveland, 1953), and **52,** Ken Boyer (St. Louis, 1964), two of the six third basemen who have been named MVPs. (Boyer was with the White Sox in 1967–68 when this picture was taken.) Rosen was the first unanimous choice. The other four third basemen MVPs were Bob Elliott (Boston Braves, 1947), Joe Torre (St. Louis, 1971), Brooks Robinson (Baltimore, 1964) and Harmon Killebrew (Minnesota, 1969). (Killebrew played 105 games at third and 80 at first base in 1969.) Gil McDougald (New York Yankees, 1951), Dick Allen (Philadelphia, 1964), Bob Horner (Atlanta, 1978), and John Castino (Minnesota, 1979) are the only four third basemen to be named Rookie of the Year. (Castino shared his award with Toronto shortstop Alfredo Griffin.) **53.** Billy Martin. Martin established a record with 12 hits in 24 times at bat in the 1953 World Series. Babe Ruth's 10 hits in 1928 were the most ever in a four-game World Series.

54. Jim Bottomley. Playing for the Cardinals, Reds and Browns between 1922 and 1937, first baseman Bottomley posted a .310 career batting average. During his final season, while appearing mostly as a pinch-hitter, Bottomley managed the eighth-place

Browns for 79 games of which he won 21 and lost 58 for a .266 percentage. **55.** Luke Appling. Playing shortstop for 20 years with the White Sox (1930–50), Appling batted .310, the same as Bottomley. In a brief managerial career in 1967, Appling took over the tenth place Kansas City Athletics from Alvin Dark with 40 games to go. He won ten and lost 30 for a .250 percentage. **56.** Honus Wagner, sliding home in this picture. In 21 seasons with Louisville and Pittsburgh (1897–1917), Wagner batted .328. During his final season, he took over the Pirates for five games, winning one and losing four for a .200 career percentage as a manager. Jack Barry, second baseman and playing manager of the Red Sox in 1917, had the best percentage of men who managed for one full year only—his team won 90, lost 62 and finished second to Chicago with a .592 mark. Preston Gomez, born April 20, 1923, in Central Preston, Cuba, is the only major league manager born in this century outside the continental United States. Gomez managed San Diego in 1969–72, Houston in 1974–75, and Chicago (NL) 1980.

57. Walter Johnson, 21 years with the Washington Senators, 1907–27. **58.** Ted Lyons, 21 years with the Chicago White Sox, 1923–46. **59.** Urban (Red) Faber, 20 years with the Chicago White Sox, 1914–33. The fourth man in this category is Mel Harder, 20 years with Cleveland, 1928–47. Johnson had the most wins with 416 (Lyons won 260, Faber 254 and Harder 223). Lyons started and completed 20 games in 1942, the last time this was done. (He won 14, lost 6.) Faber's 254 wins are the most by a modern pitcher who never led the league in wins. **60.** (Sad) Sam Jones. Jones pitched during 22 consecutive calendar years, 1914–35, for six teams, winning 229 and losing 217. Cy Young shares the 22-year record with Jones—from 1890 through 1911 Young pitched for five teams, both winning (511) and losing (313) more games than any other pitcher in major league history.

61. Jack Coombs, winner of three games for the Philadelphia Athletics in the 1910 World Series—the A's beat the Cubs, four games to one. (He was with Detroit in 1920 when this picture was taken.) Christy Mathewson was 3–0 for the New York Giants during their 1905 four-games-to-one Series win over the Athletics. **62.** Stan Coveleski, 3–0 for Cleveland in 1920. **63.** Harry Brecheen, 3–0 for the St. Louis Cardinals in 1946. The other four pitchers to post 3–0 records in a World Series are: Babe Adams (Pittsburgh, 1909); Lew Burdette (Milwaukee, 1957); Bob Gibson (St. Louis, 1967); Mickey Lolich (Detroit, 1968). Coombs won another World Series game for the Athletics in 1911 and a final one for Brooklyn in 1916, giving him a lifetime 5–0 Series record. **64.** Herb Pennock, the other 5–0 Series pitcher. Pennock won two in 1923, two more in 1926 and one in 1927, all for the Yankees. Lefty Gomez is the only 6–0 Series pitcher. He won one in 1932, two in 1936, two in 1937 and one in 1938, also all for the Yankees. Deacon Phillippe pitched the most innings in a single World Series—44 for Pittsburgh against Boston in the first Series in 1903. Phillippe was 3–2 (the only pitcher with five decisions in a single Series), but ended up on the losing side as the Red Sox won the eight-game Series, five games to three, with three of Boston's wins being hurled by Bill Dineen.

65. Freddie Lindstrom. Lindstrom was 18 when he played third base for the Giants in the 1924 World Series against Washington. Lindstrom batted .333, but the Giants lost the Series four games to three when a ball hit by Earl McNeeley bounced over his head in the seventh game. Tommy Brown was 17 when he hit a home run for the Dodgers off Preacher Roe, then with the Pirates, at Ebbets Field on August 30, 1945. **66.** Tony Conigliaro of the Red Sox. He passed the 100 home run mark at the age of 22 during the 1967 season. **67.** Eddie Mathews. He passed the 200 home run mark at 25 during the 1957 season. Mathews was also 22 when he passed the 100 mark, but was a few months older than Conigliaro. Mathews' 30 home runs on the road with the 1953 Milwaukee Braves is the National League record. (He hit only 17 at home that year.) Babe Ruth set the American League record with 32 home runs on the road when he hit 60 in 1927. **68.** Bill Bruton. As a Brave, Bruton led the National League in stolen bases with 26 in 1953, 34 in 1954 and 25 in 1955. (This photo was taken while Bruton was with Detroit between 1961 and 1964.)

69. Eddie Collins. Collins, sixth on the all-time hit list with 3311 and Ty Cobb, first with 4191, are the only two left-hitting and right-throwing players to collect 3000 or more hits. Collins' hit total is the most by a player who never led the league in hits. **70.** Stuffy McInnis, first baseman on the Philadelphia Athletics' "$100,000 infield" during the years before World War I. Jack Barry was the shortstop and Frank (Home Run) Baker was the third baseman. Baker's home runs on October 16 and 17 in the 1911 World Series against the Giants were the first in a Series by one player on consecutive days. The A's won the Series four games to two. **71.** Heinie Zimmerman. He led the National League with 14 home runs and a .372 batting average in 1912, but revised figures gave Honus Wagner of the Pirates 102 RBIs while reducing Zimmerman's total to 98.

72. Connie Mack, manager of Pittsburgh, 1894–96 and the Philadelphia Athletics for 50 years, 1901–50. In 53 years Mack won nine pennants, but compiled an overall percentage of .484. **73.** Bucky Harris, shown here during his playing days. As a manager of several teams for 29 years—between 1924 and 1956—Harris had an overall winning percentage of .493 and won three pennants. The third manager in this group is Jimmy Dykes. Dykes had a .478 percentage as a manager over 21 seasons between 1934 and 1961. He won 1407 games, but never won a pennant, or even finished second. Wilbert Robinson, manager of the Baltimore American League team in 1902 and the Brooklyn Dodgers for 18 seasons, 1914–31, won 1397 games and lost 1395 for a career winning percentage of .5003. **74.** Casey Stengel, manager of a minor league team at Oakland in 1948 and Manager-of-the-Year with the Yankees in 1949. George Moriarty was the only major league player, manager and umpire. He played for several teams between 1903 and 1916, managed the Detroit Tigers in 1927 and 1928 (to fourth-place and sixth-place finishes) and was an American League umpire during the other years between 1917 and 1940.

75. Art Nehf. With the Giants, Nehf won one game in every World Series from 1921 through 1924. **76.** Howard Ehmke. Pitching for the Athletics, Ehmke gave up Ruth's first home run in 1927. **77.** Tom Zachary. Shown here pitching for Brooklyn in the 1930s, Zachary was a Washington Senator in 1927 when Ruth tagged him for his 60th. Ehmke struck out a record 13 Cubs for the

Athletics in the first game of the 1929 World Series; the A's went on to win the Series four games to one. The Dodgers' Carl Erskine broke Ehmke's record by striking out 14 Yankees in the third game of the 1953 Series, but the Yankees still won the Series four games to two. (St. Louis' Bob Gibson set the current record by striking out 17 Tigers in the first game of the 1968 Series.) Ed Walsh led the American League in losses with an overall 18–20 record for the 1910 Chicago White Sox while pitching seven shutouts. Mel Stottlemyre of the Yankees had seven shutouts in 1972 while leading the league in losses with a 14–18 record. Also in 1910, Walsh became the only pitcher ever to lead the league in losses and lowest earned-run average in the same year—his ERA was 1.27. Ray Sadecki of the San Francisco Giants had six shutouts while compiling a 12–18 mark in 1968; no National League pitcher has ever thrown more shutouts while leading his league in losses.

78. Jackie Robinson. In 1949 he led the National League in stolen bases with 37 for Brooklyn while winning his one batting championship with a .342 average. **79.** Snuffy Stirnweiss. Stirnweiss won his one batting title for the Yankees in 1945 with a .309 average while leading the American League with 33 stolen bases. Stirnweiss' career average of .268 is the lowest of any player who ever won just one batting title. **80.** Pete Runnels, American League batting champion for Boston in 1962 with a .326 average, was traded to Houston before the 1963 season. Detroit's Harvey Kuenn won the American League batting title in 1959 with a .353 average and was traded to Cleveland the following year. Chicago Cub Bill Madlock won his second batting title in 1976 with a .339 average and was traded to San Francisco before the following season. Billy North's 75 stolen bases for Oakland in 1976 are the most by an American League player since Cobb's 96 in 1915. Clyde Milan, a Washington Senator for 16 years (1907–22), stole the most career bases, 495, of any man who played for only one team; he is tenth on the all-time stolen base list.

81. Robin Roberts, 28–7 with the 1952 Philadelphia Phillies. **82.** Don Newcombe, 27–7 with the 1956 Brooklyn Dodgers, the year he won both the MVP and Cy Young awards. **83.** Dean Chance, 20–9 with the 1964 Los Angeles Angels; his 20 wins include 11 shutouts, most by an American League pitcher during the 1960s. The two National Leaguers to have ten or more shutouts in a year during the 1960s were Sandy Koufax with 11 for the Dodgers in 1963 (his overall record was 25–5) and Bob Gibson with 13 for the Cardinals in 1968 (22–9 overall). During his 17 years with the Cardinals (1959–75), Gibson made 303 consecutive appearances as a starter, the major league record. Mel Stottlemyre set the American League record with 272 consecutive appearances as a starter during his 11 years with the Yankees, 1964–74. Bert Blyleven, born in Zeist, Holland, on April 6, 1951, easily has the most career wins, 148 through 1979 for Minnesota, Texas and Pittsburgh, of any pitcher born outside the Western Hemisphere in a non-English-speaking country.

84. Roger Peckinpaugh. Peckinpaugh committed his record eight errors playing for Washington against Pittsburgh in 1925; the Senators lost the Series four games to three. With New York in the 1914 season, Peckinpaugh, age 23, replaced Frank Chance with 17 games to go, becoming baseball's youngest manager. He stayed with New York as a player but was replaced as manager by Wild Bill Donovan for the 1915 season. **85.** Joe Sewell, charged with six errors playing for Cleveland against Brooklyn in the 1920 World Series, won by the Indians five games to two. Honus Wagner is the other Hall of Fame shortstop who committed six errors in a single World Series; his came in the first Series, 1903, which Wagner's Pirates lost to Boston, five games to three. Sewell's 1103 consecutive games during his 14-year career (1920–33) are *not* a record for shortstops; Everett Scott played in 1307 consecutive games at short during his 13-year career with five teams, 1914–26. **86.** Billy Rogell, shortstop for the Tigers during the 1930s, shown here in a Cub uniform during 1940, his last major league year. Rogell became a Detroit alderman after retiring from baseball and now has an expressway in Detroit named after him. **87.** Arky Vaughan. He hit .385 and led the National League for Pittsburgh in 1935. The modern American League record for shortstops was set by Chicago's Luke Appling with a .388 league-leading average in 1936.

88. George Uhle, winner of 200 (and loser of 166) games during 17 seasons (1919–36) for four teams. His career batting average of .288 in 1363 times at bat is the highest for any pitcher with over 500 times at bat. Erv Brame of Pittsburgh hit .306 in 396 times at bat over five seasons (1928–32), the highest average for any pitcher with over 300 times at bat. **89.** Dutch Ruether. Ruether hit two triples for Cincinnati against the White Sox in the first game of the 1919 World Series. Cincinnati won the game 9–1 and the "Black Sox" Series, five games to three. **90.** Waite Hoyt. Pitching for many teams during a 21-year career, 1918–38, Hoyt came to bat 1287 times without hitting a home run. Dutch Leonard, pitching for four teams between 1933 and 1953, came to bat 1054 times in 20 seasons without a homer. Baltimore's Dave McNally became the only pitcher to hit a grand slam home run in the World Series when he connected in the third game of the 1970 Series against Cincinnati. Baltimore won the game 9–3 and the Series four games to one. **91.** Jim Bagby, Sr. His World Series home run came in the fifth game of the 1920 Series for Cleveland against Brooklyn. Cleveland won the game 8–1 and the Series five games to two. Rosy Ryan of the New York Giants was the first National League pitcher to hit a World Series home run; he connected in the third game in 1924 against the Senators. The Giants won the game 6–4, but lost the Series four games to three.

92. Charlie Robertson. He pitched his perfect game on April 30, 1922, for the Chicago White Sox, beating Detroit 2–0. **93.** Jim Bunning, pitcher of the next regular-season perfect game. He threw his for the Phillies against the Mets on June 21, 1964, winning 6–0. (He was with Detroit earlier in his career when this photo was taken.) **94.** Cleveland's Johnny Allen. His 15–1 record and .938 percentage in 1937 is the best ever recorded by an American League pitcher with at least 15 decisions. Pittsburgh's Roy Face, 18–1 and a .947 percentage in 1959, set the major league mark. **95.** Dan Bankhead, the first black pitcher in the National League. He pitched 10 innings for Brooklyn in 1947. San Francisco Giant Jim Barr retired a record 41 consecutive batters while pitching two straight shutouts in 1972—neither was a no-hitter. Cy Young and Early Wynn are the only 300-game winners to lead the league in losses. Young did it with the Red Sox in 1906 with a 13–21 record; Wynn's 8–17 mark with Washington in 1944 led the American League in losses.

96. Centerfielder Happy Felsch. **97.** First baseman Chick Gandil. **98.** Third baseman Buck Weaver. **99.** Shortstop Swede Risberg. **100.** Manager Kid Gleason. Weaver established a record for hits by a switch-hitter in 1920 with 210. The other four players banned were pitchers Ed Cicotte and Lefty Williams, outfielder "Shoeless" Joe Jackson and reserve infielder Fred McMullin. Manager Gleason continued to manage the team through the 1923 season.

101. Hal Chase. Chase won the batting title with a .339 average for the 1916 Cincinnati Reds. **102.** Lou Criger, a major league catcher for several teams over 16 seasons, 1896–1912. Chase, Criger and "Shoeless" Joe Jackson are the only three players who received votes in the initial 1936 Hall of Fame election who are still not in the Hall. New York Met Cleon Jones was the last left-throwing and right-batting player to hit .300; he had a .340 average in 1969 and hit .319 in 1971. **103.** Jim Thorpe, who played most of his six years in the majors, 1913–19, with the New York Giants, was with Cincinnati on May 2, 1917, when he drove in the tenth-inning run that gave Red pitcher Fred Toney a no-hit win over Cub Jim Vaughan, who had also pitched nine innings of no-hit ball. Running back Vic Janowicz, 1950 Heisman Trophy winner at Ohio State, was the only Heisman winner to play baseball in the major leagues. He played 83 games as a catcher, third baseman and outfielder with Pittsburgh in 1953–54. **104.** Hank Thompson. Thompson came to the major leagues with the St. Louis Browns for 27 games in 1947; returning to the majors in 1949, he spent eight seasons with the Giants, participating in the four-game sweep over Cleveland in the 1954 Series.

105. Wilcy Moore. Moore, an early relief specialist, had only six major league seasons, 1927–33, and spent one and a half of them with the Red Sox. He went nine innings to win the fourth game of the 1927 Series as the Yankees swept Pittsburgh. In the fourth game of the 1932 Series, Moore relieved Johnny Allen in the first inning and pitched five and a third innings to win the game 13–6 and preserve the Yankee sweep with the help of a save by Herb Pennock. **106.** Earle (The Kentucky Colonel) Combs. Yankee Bob Grim became the only 20-game winner to be named Rookie of the Year following his 20–6 season in 1954. **107.** Bob Shawkey, winner of 198 games in 15 years (1913–27), mostly for the Yankees, including the first game played at Yankee Stadium in 1923, when he pitched and batted the Yankees to a 4–2 win over the Red Sox.

108. Harry Heilmann, American League batting champion in 1921 (.394), 1923 (.403), 1925 (.393) and 1927 (.398). **109.** Bob Meusel, Yankee leftfielder in 1927. He "hit for the cycle" in 1921, 1922 and 1928, all for the Yankees. Babe Herman is the only National Leaguer to hit for the cycle three times. He did it twice for the Dodgers in 1931 and once with the Cubs in 1933. **110.** Max Bishop. He played 53 consecutive games without an error in 1932. Baltimore Oriole Jerry Adair broke this record with 89 consecutive errorless games at second base in 1964–65. **111.** Cy Williams, co-leader of the National League in home runs in 1927. Chicago Cub Hack Wilson shared the league leadership with Williams.

112. Babe Ruth, thrown out stealing in the ninth inning of the seventh game of the 1926 World Series. The St. Louis Cardinals won the game 3-2 and the Series, 4-3. **113.** Jesse (Pop) Haines, winning Cardinal pitcher in that game, with the help of a famous relief appearance by Grover Cleveland Alexander, who struck out Tony Lazzeri with the bases loaded in the seventh inning and preserved the win the rest of the way. **114.** Frankie Frisch. Ruth and Frisch (then with the Cardinals) hit the only home runs in the first All Star game at Chicago's Comiskey Park on July 6, 1933. The American League won, 4-2. Ruth's 177 runs in 1921 are the most scored in one season by any player during the 20th century. Also in 1921, Ruth had his only 200 hit, 50 home run year. He led the major leagues with 59 homers out of 204 hits in all. Chicago Cub Hack Wilson, with 56 home runs in 208 hits in 1930, and Philadelphia Athletic Jimmie Foxx, with 58 homers in 213 hits in 1932 are the only other two players to have a 200 hit, 50 home run year. Bob (Fats) Fothergill of the Detroit Tigers got the most pinch hits in a year during the 1920s with 19 in 1929.

115. Rube Waddell. Pitching for the Athletics against Boston, Waddell was on the losing side of Cy Young's 3-0 perfect game on May 5, 1904. Waddell batted for himself as the 27th man to face Young that day and was retired to end the game. In every other nine inning perfect game in this century the losing pitcher was removed for a pinch hitter before his final turn at bat. Waddell struck out 200 batters six times, but Walter Johnson did this seven times for Washington for the American League record, and Tom Seaver has done it ten times through 1979 for the major league record. **116.** Freddie Fitzsimmons, a Giant for a bit more than 12 of his 19 seasons in the major leagues between 1925 and 1943. **117.** Hal Schumacher, a Giant for all of his 13 major league seasons (1931-46). They were teammates on the 1933 and 1936 pennant-winning Giants teams, beating Washington in the 1933 Series, four games to one, but losing to the Yankees in the 1936 Series, four games to two. In 1929 Fitzsimmons shut out the Reds in four consecutive starting appearances against them—June 8 (3-0), June 11 (9-0), July 7 (8-0) and July 30 (3-0). Oddly, these were the only four shutouts Fitzsimmons recorded that year. **118.** Masanori Murakami, a relief pitcher for the San Francisco Giants in 1964 and 1965. He compiled a 5-1 record with nine saves in 54 appearances.

119. Steve Carlton. With the Phillies, Carlton led the National League in wins in 1972 with a 27-10 record and in losses in 1973 with a 13-20 mark. Carlton won the Cy Young Award in 1972 when the Phillies were last in the Eastern Division of the National League. **120.** Bob Friend. With the Pirates, Friend led the National League in wins in 1958 with a 22-14 record; his 8-19 record led the league in losses the following year. **121.** Hal Newhouser. With the Tigers, Newhouser led the American League in wins in 1946 with a 26-9 mark; his 17-17 record led the AL in losses the following year. In 1944 and 1945, Newhouser won consecutive Most Valuable Player Awards, the only pitcher to do this. The other six pitchers to lead the league in wins one year and in losses the next were: Al Orth (New York, American League) 27-17 in 1906, 13-21 in 1907; Dick Rudolph (Boston, National League) 27-10 in 1914, 21-19 in 1915; Eddie Cicotte (Chicago, American League) 28-12 in 1917, 12-19 in 1918; Eddie Rommel (Philadelphia, American League) 27-13 in 1922, 18-19 in 1923; Bob Lemon (Cleveland, American League) 23-11 in 1950, 17-14 in

1951; Robin Roberts (Philadelphia, National League) 23-14 in 1955, 19-18 in 1956. Jim Lonborg of the Boston Red Sox gave up the fewest hits, four, in two consecutive World Series complete game victories. In the 1967 Series, Longborg gave the Cardinals one hit while beating them 5-0 in the second game, and three hits while beating them 3-1 in the fifth game. The Cardinals won the Series four games to three.

122. Pete Gray. In his only season Gray batted .218 in 77 games with six doubles and two triples among his 51 hits. **123.** Paul O'Dea. O'Dea played for the Cleveland Indians in 1944-45. Pitching, he compiled a 0-0 record in four games. As an outfielder-first baseman, he batted .272 in 163 games. **124.** Hugh Mulcahy of the Phillies, the first player to be drafted in World War II. In six years before the War, Mulcahy won 42 and lost 82 games for the Phillies. Returning after the War, Mulcahy was 3-7 in 23 games in 1945-47. **125.** Boston Braves outfielder Tommy Holmes. Holmes led the National League in home runs in 1945 with 28 and had the fewest strikeouts, nine, among regular players.

126 & 127. Paul and Lloyd Waner. They hit many back-to-back home runs playing for Pittsburgh between 1927 and 1940. They were both retired when Chicago Cub shortstop Jimmy Cooney executed his unassisted triple play at Pittsburgh on May 30, 1927. Washington Senator shortstop Ron Hansen executed the only unassisted triple play in a night game (in fact the only unassisted triple play, day or night, since the beginning of night baseball) at Cleveland on July 30, 1968. **128 & 129.** Phil and Joe Niekro, the only brothers to pitch against each other in a National League game. On July 4, 1967, they pitched against each other in a game between the Braves and the Cubs which the Braves (with Phil pitching) won 8-3. In 1970 San Francisco's Gaylord Perry led the National League in wins with a 23-13 record and 41 games started, the same year his brother, Jim, led the American League in wins with a 24-12 record and 40 games started for the Minnesota Twins.

130. Ted Williams. **131.** Rogers Hornsby. Williams won his two triple crowns for the Red Sox in 1942 (.356 batting average, 36 home runs and 137 runs batted in) and 1947 (.343 batting average, 32 home runs and 114 runs batted in). Hornsby won his two with the St. Louis Cardinals in 1922 (.401 batting average, 42 home runs and 152 runs batted in) and 1925 (.403 batting average, 39 home runs and 143 runs batted in). Williams' .344 career batting average, sixth on the all-time list, is the highest by a player who played his whole career with one team. Hornsby, a second baseman, got a league-leading 250 hits in 1922, the only time a non-outfielder and non-first baseman surpassed 240. Included, as listed above, were a league-leading 42 home runs—the only time a 240-plus hit player led the league in home runs. Detroit's Hank Greenberg got 39 of his league-leading 58 home runs at home in 1938, the most ever hit by a player in his home park in one year. Max Carey played 20 years, 1910-29, for Pittsburgh and Brooklyn. During that time he played in only one World Series, in 1925 as Pittsburgh beat Washington four games to three. Carey's .458 batting average in that Series gives him the highest World Series batting average of any player who played 20 or more years in the major leagues.

132. Ty Cobb. **133.** George Sisler. With Detroit in 1911, Cobb batted .420 with 248 hits; in 1922 with the St. Louis Browns, Sisler batted .420 with 246 hits. Cobb led the American League in stolen bases with 83 in 1911; Sisler led in 1922 with 51. Cobb won his triple crown in 1909 with a .377 batting average, nine home runs and 115 runs batted in. The nine home runs are the fewest and his 76 stolen bases that year are the most by a triple crown winner. Sisler's son Dick played eight years (1946–53) for three teams. A first baseman-outfielder, his career batting average was .276. Sisler's other son, Dave, pitched for four teams, 1956–62. His career record was 38–44. **134.** Heinie Manush. He collected 241 hits with the Browns in 1928. His .378 batting average and 14 strikeouts were the lowest ever recorded by any player with more than 240 hits in one year.

135. Fred Merkle. With the Giants in a late-season game against their rivals, the Cubs, Merkle failed to touch second base, allowing himself to be forced out in a confusing game-ending play, costing the Giants a game they had apparently won. When the Cubs tied the Giants for the pennant and then won the playoff, Merkle was blamed for the defeat and ridiculed by press and fans alike. **136.** Joe Tinker (left) and Johnny Evers (right), two thirds of the famous Tinker-to-Evers-to-Chance infield. Shortstop Tinker stole 304 bases for the Cubs between 1902 and 1912 and another 32 with Cincinnati in the National League and Chicago in the Federal League in 1913–15, giving him 336 for his career. Second baseman Evers stole 291 bases for the Cubs between 1902 and 1913 and another 33 for three other teams between 1914 and 1917, giving him 324 overall. First baseman Frank Chance, with 404 stolen bases for the Cubs between 1898 and 1912, (and one more with New York in the American League in 1913) is the all-time Cub stolen base leader. Detroit's Charlie Gehringer had separate streaks of 511 and 504 consecutive games at second base during his 19-year career between 1924 and 1942.

137. Leon (Goose) Goslin. He led the American League in runs batted in in 1924 with 129. Roy Sievers (114 in 1957) and Frank Howard (126 in 1970) are the other two Senators to lead the league in this department. **138.** Eddie Yost. He played 829 consecutive games at third for Washington between 1950 and 1955. His 151 walks in 1956 was the most in the major leagues during the 1950s. Houston's Jimmy Wynn had the most walks in one year in the 1960s—148 in 1969. **139.** James (Mickey) Vernon. Outfielder Sam Rice struck out only 275 times in 20 years, 1915–34, with Washington and (one year) Cleveland. **140.** Joe Judge.

141. Joe Jackson. His career average, .356, is the third all-time highest and best by a player who never led the league in that category. Jackson hit 26 triples for Cleveland in 1912. **142.** Kiki Cuyler, who hit 26 triples for Pittsburgh in 1925. **143.** Larry Doyle, the only infielder to hit 25 or more triples in one season, had 25 for the New York Giants in 1911. The other three players in this category are: Owen Wilson, the all-time single-season leader in triples, who hit 36 for Pittsburgh in 1912; Tommy Long, who hit 25 for the St. Louis Cardinals in 1915; Sam Crawford, the only player to do this twice. Crawford hit 25 triples for Detroit in 1903 and 26 for Detroit in 1914. Pittsburgh's Tommy Leach was the only player to hit four triples in a single World Series. He hit

four for Pittsburgh in the 1903 Series, which the Pirates lost to Boston, five games to three.

144. Ed Cicotte, 21–10 with the 1920 White Sox. 1920 was Cicotte's final year in baseball before he was banned "for life" because of his involvement in the fixing of the 1919 World Series. Claude (Lefty) Williams, 22–14 for the 1920 White Sox, is one of the other two men in this category—for the same reason. Sandy Koufax, who retired from baseball because of an elbow injury following a 27–9 year with the Dodgers in 1966, is the only other pitcher to win 20 or more games in his final season. Koufax pitched no-hitters in four consecutive years; against the Mets on June 30, 1962, winning 5–0; against the Giants on May 11, 1963, winning 8–0; against the Phillies on June 4, 1964, winning 3–0; and a perfect game against the Cubs on September 9, 1965, winning 1–0. **145.** Bob Feller, credited with the win in the 1946 All Star game, won by the American League 12–0. Feller teamed with pitchers Hal Newhouser and Jack Kramer to pitch a combined three-hitter. **146.** Harry Byrd, Rookie of the Year with the Philadelphia Athletics in 1952 with a 15–15 record. (He was with the Yankees in 1954 when this photo was taken.) Dazzy Vance, who won 197 games while losing 140 during his 16-year career with several teams (1915–35), was 31 when he won his first game in 1922 for Brooklyn, the oldest of any Hall of Fame pitcher to win as many as 190 major league games. Baltimore Oriole Jim Palmer is the only pitcher to pitch more than 3000 innings without giving up a grand slam. Through the 1979 season, including 3275 innings pitched, Palmer had never been tagged for a home run with the bases full.

147. Babe Herman, 241 hits for Brooklyn in 1930. **148.** Chuck Klein, 250 hits for the Philadelphia Phillies in 1930. **149.** Lefty O'Doul, 254 hits for the Phillies in 1929. (He was with Brooklyn in 1931–33 when this photo was taken.) Klein and Herman were both beaten for the 1930 National League leadership in hits by Bill Terry's 254 for the New York Giants. O'Doul walked 76 times in 1929, the most for any player with 240 or more hits, but stole only two bases, the fewest for any player with 240 or more hits. Jesse Burkett had 240 hits for the Cleveland team in the National League in 1896, the only 19th-century player to reach that total. Luke Sewell, catcher for four teams for 20 years (1921–42), had the fewest home runs, 20, of any non-pitcher to play an entire career of 20 or more years in the 20th century.

150. Al Simmons. **151.** Hack Wilson. **152.** Lou Gehrig (right, with Zeke Bonura). Simmons drove in 165 runs for the 1930 Philadelphia Athletics; Wilson drove in an all-time record 190 runs for the 1930 Chicago Cubs; Gehrig drove in 174 runs for the 1930 Yankees. Chuck Klein of the Phillies drove in 170 runs in 1930. Simmons, with the A's in 1925, got 253 hits, the most ever by a right-handed batter. Gehrig's 1991 runs batted in during 17 years with the Yankees (1923–39), are the most by a player who played his whole career with one team. His four home runs in the 1928 World Series, swept by the Yankees over the Cardinals, are the most in a four-game Series. Sam Thompson was the only 19th-century player to drive in 165 or more runs in a year. He did it twice: 166 for Detroit in 1887 and 165 for Philadelphia in 1895, both National League teams. Pittsburgh's Ralph Kiner is the only player to hit home runs in three consecutive All Star games; he connected in 1949, 1950 and 1951.

153. Dizzy Dean. Earl Averill of Cleveland hit the drive that broke Dean's toe and brought his career to an end within a few years. 154. Brooklyn's Hugh Casey. Casey lost the third and fourth games of the 1941 World Series on October 4 and 5 to the Yankees by scores of 2-1 and 7-4. In both cases, he was pitching in relief; the Yankees won the Series four games to one. In 1947, Casey won the third and fourth games against the Yankees on October 2 and 3 by scores of 9-8 and 3-2, again pitching in relief. Even so, the Yankees won the Series again, four games to three. 155. St. Louis Cardinal pitcher Mort Cooper; he lost the 1942 and 1943 All Star games for the National League by scores of 3-1 and 5-3—in both cases he was the starting pitcher. In the 1942 Series, Cooper was 0-1 as St. Louis beat the Yankees four games to one; in the 1943 Series, Cooper was 1-1 as the Yankees beat the Cardinals in return, four games to one. 156. Paul Derringer. He won the fourth and seventh games of the 1940 World Series as the Reds beat the Tigers four games to three; he was also the starting and winning pitcher in the 1940 All Star game which was won by the National League, 4-0. The other five pitchers who won an All Star and World Series game in the same year were: Carl Hubbell, 1936; Lefty Gomez, 1937; Spec Shea, 1947; Bob Friend, 1960; and Sandy Koufax, 1965. Warren Spahn, winner of 363 games during his 21-year career, 1942-65 with the Braves, Mets and Giants, was 25 when he won his first game in 1946, the oldest first win of any 300-game winner.

157. Richie Ashburn, National League batting leader with the last-place 1958 Phillies. His average was .350. 158. Detroit's Norm Cash. His league-leading .361 average in 1961 was 90 points higher than his career mark of .271, the biggest such margin in history. 159. Nap Lajoie, 1901 American League batting champion with the Philadelphia Athletics; he had an AL record .422 average, 82 points higher than the runner-up, Baltimore's Mike Donlin. 160. St. Louis Cardinal Joe Medwick, winner of a triple crown in 1937 with a .374 average, 31 home runs and 154 runs batted in, a year he also led National League outfielders in fielding. Lajoie also led the league in fielding in 1901 when he added the triple crown to his record .422 average—he hit 14 home runs and drove in 125 runs. Cleveland's Elmer Flick won the American League batting title with a .306 average in 1905; his career average was .315, which makes him the only batting champion with a career average higher than his league-leading season's average.

161. Mickey Mantle. 162. Jimmie Foxx. Mantle and Foxx both hit 50 home runs and still didn't lead the league. Mantle's 54 with the Yankees in 1961 was second to Roger Maris's 61; Foxx's 50 with the Red Sox in 1938 was second to Hank Greenberg's 58. Mantle and Foxx are also the only two players to hit 50 or more home runs and win a batting title: Mantle hit 52 in 1956, his triple crown year, and won the batting title with a .353 average. Foxx led the American League in hitting with a .349 average in 1938. Mantle's 536 career home runs, sixth on the all-time list, are the most for a player who played his whole career with one team; Foxx hit 50 or more home runs for two different franchises—58 in 1932 for the Philadelphia Athletics and 50 in 1938 for the Boston Red Sox. 163. Bob Nieman. With the St. Louis Browns in 1951, Nieman hit home runs in his first two major league at bats, the only time

this was ever done. Mantle has the most home runs of any switch-hitter; second all-time switch-hitting home run producer is Reggie Smith with 280 through the 1979 season with the Red Sox and Dodgers. Bill (Moose) Skowron of the Yankees is the only man ever to hit a grand slam home run in the seventh game of a World Series; he connected in 1956 against the Dodgers as the Yankees won the game 9-0 and the Series four games to three.

164. Johnny Frederick. His six pinch-hit home runs for the 1932 Brooklyn Dodgers are the major league record. 165. Joe Cronin. He set the American League record with five pinch-hit home runs for the Red Sox in 1943. Cronin drove in at least one run in a record 12 games between June 27 and July 9, 1939. 166. Dusty Rhodes. Rhodes had 55 career pinch hits in 260 times at bat over seven years with the New York and San Francisco Giants (1952-59), but is best remembered for pinch-hitting a three-run homer to win the first game of the 1954 World Series, then coming back in the second game to drive in a run with a pinch single and another run when he stayed in the game and hit his second World Series home run for New York; in the third game Rhodes delivered two more runs with a bases-loaded pinch single. The Giants swept Cleveland 4-0 in the Series. 167. Elmer Valo. During 20 major league seasons (1940-61) with several teams, Valo got 90 pinch hits in 386 times at bat as a pinch hitter. He delivered his three bases-loaded triples for the Athletics in May, 1949. Doc Miller, with 20 pinch hits for the 1913 Phillies, was the first player to have 20 in one year; Smokey Burgess was the only player to have two 20-pinch-hit years with 20 in 1965 and 21 in 1966, both times with the White Sox. 168. John Burnett. Playing for Cleveland against the Athletics on July 10, 1932, Burnett had a record nine hits in 11 times at bat in an 18-inning game.

169. Truett (Rip) Sewell of the Pirates had one of his famous high-arched "ephus" pitches tagged for a home run by Ted Williams in the 1946 All Star Game. 170. Hank Borowy, 108-82 in ten major league years (1942-51). He played on Yankee pennant winners in 1942 and 1943, and with the Cubs' first-place team in 1945. In 1945, Borowy was 21-7 overall, 10-5 with the Yankees and 11-2 with the Cubs, the only 20-game winner spread over two leagues. 171. Bobby Shantz. Shantz' 2.45 ERA was the American League's best in 1957. 172. Ron Perranoski. He led the National League in games pitched in with the Dodgers in 1962 (70), 1963 (69), and 1967 (70). With the Minnesota Twins, he led the American League in saves with 31 in 1969 and 34 in 1970. 173. Firpo Marberry. With the Washington Senators Marberry led the American League in games pitched in in 1924 (50), 1925 (55), 1926 (64), 1928 (48), 1929 (49) and 1932 (54). (He was with Detroit later on when this picture was taken.)

174. Lynwood (Schoolboy) Rowe, who won 16 consecutive games for Detroit in 1934. 175. Paul (Dizzy) Trout whose 2.12 ERA led the American League in 1944. Hal Newhouser led the AL in ERA in 1945 and 1946 with ERAs 1.81 and 1.94 respectively. 176. Lon Warneke, who won 22 for the Cubs in 1932, 22 again in 1934 and 20 in 1935. 177. Burleigh Grimes. Grimes compiled an overall record of 270-212 in 19 seasons between 1916 and 1934 with several teams. He was the last of the legal spitballers to retire, 14 years after the pitch had been outlawed with a dispensation given

to active pitchers then using the doctored pitch to be able to continue to do so until the end of their careers. Carl Hubbell's 1.66 ERA with the Giants in 1933 is the lowest of any left-hander to pitch at least 300 innings—Hubbell pitched 308.2. Pud Galvin won the most one-sided no-hitter ever by the score of 18-0 pitching for the Buffalo National League team against Detroit on August 4, 1884.

178. Duke Snider. Snider's 11 career World Series home runs are the most by a non-Yankee. Mickey Mantle (18), Babe Ruth (15), Yogi Berra (12) and Lou Gehrig (ten) are the only other players to hit ten or more World Series home runs. **179.** Carl Furillo. Besides Furillo, Mel Ott, Hack Wilson and Jim (Junior) Gilliam were the only players to hit the sign. **180.** Van Lingle Mungo. Chuck Hiller of the San Francisco Giants was the first National Leaguer to hit a World Series grand slam; he connected in the fourth game of the 1962 Series against the Yankees. The Giants won the game 7-3 but lost the Series, 4-3. **181.** Roy Campanella. Campanella's 41 home runs in 1953 was the record for catchers until it was broken by Johnny Bench of Cincinnati with 45 in 1970. Campanella stole 25 bases during his ten-year career, 1948-57. The only Hall of Fame catcher with fewer steals was Branch Rickey, elected to the Hall because of his achievements as a baseball executive. Rickey played in the major leagues for four seasons, 1905-07, and 1914, for the New York and St. Louis American League teams. In 119 games, 66 as a catcher, Rickey stole eight bases, the least of any major league catcher in the Hall of Fame.

182. Hank Gowdy. Gowdy hit .545 for the Boston National League team in 1914 as they swept the Series from the Philadelphia Athletics. In 1928, as the Yankees swept the Cardinals, Lou Gehrig tied Gowdy's mark, and Babe Ruth demolished it with a .625 average—ten hits in 16 times at bat. **183.** Larry French. **184.** Mickey Owen. Owen's pinch-hit home run came in the 1942 All Star Game at New York, won by the American League, 3-1. **185.** Moe Berg. Billy Sullivan, primarily a catcher with several teams for 16 seasons (1899-1916), had the lowest batting average, .212, of any 15-year major leaguer.

186. Lou Boudreau. Boudreau, shortstop and manager of the World Champion 1948 Cleveland Indians—winners in the Series over the Braves 4-2—stole 51 bases, least by an American League Hall of Fame shortstop, during his 15-year career with Cleveland and Boston (1938-52). Chicago Cub Ernie Banks, who divided his 19-year career (1953-71) between shortstop (1125 games) and first base (1259 games) stole 50 bases. **187.** Bill Virdon. Virdon was Rookie of the Year with the St. Louis Cardinals in 1955 and Manager of the Year with Pittsburgh in 1972. The other two Rookies of the Year to become major league managers were: Alvin Dark, Rookie of the Year with the Giants in 1948 and manager of several teams, 1961-77; Frank Robinson, Rookie of the Year with Cincinnati in 1956 and manager of the Cleveland Indians, 1975-77. **188.** Earle (Greasy) Neale. Neale played for the 1919 Cincinnati Reds in the World Series against the White Sox; he later coached Washington and Jefferson in the Rose Bowl. The other two men to appear in a World Series and a Rose Bowl were Chuck Esseghian and Jackie Jensen. Billy Southworth managed the 1943

and 1944 St. Louis Cardinals, winning two pennants with 105-49 records each year. Fred Clarke of Pittsburgh won the National League pennant by the biggest margin—27 1/2 games in 1902; Joe McCarthy of the Yankees won the American League pennant by the biggest margin—19 1/2 games in 1936. **189.** Miller Huggins. Art Fletcher managed the last 11 games of the 1929 season.

190. Pepper Martin. He hit .500 (12 for 24) in seven games in the 1931 World Series as the Cardinals beat the Athletics 4-3. The Yankee's Johnny Lindell hit .500 (9 for 18) in the 1947 World Series as the Yankees beat Brooklyn 4-3. They are the only two players to bat .500 in a seven-game World Series. **191.** Stanley (Frenchy) Bordagaray. **192.** Ben Chapman. His 61 stolen bases for the 1931 Yankees were the most by a player in one year during the 1930s. **193.** Estel Crabtree, who played eight years as an outfielder for Cincinnati and St. Louis (1929-44), batting .281 in 489 games, was born in Crabtree, Ohio.

194. Willie Mays. **195.** Rudy York. With the Giants (then in New York), Mays had 24 stolen bases in 1955 when he hit 51 home runs for the highest stolen-base total of any player with 50 or more home runs in a year. Playing for Detroit, York set the major league record with 18 home runs in August, 1937; Mays set the National League mark with 17 in one month in August, 1965 for the San Francisco Giants. **196.** Roger Maris, shown here during his early years with the Kansas City Athletics. Maris had no stolen bases in 1961, the year he set the record with 61 home runs. Maris's .269 batting average was the lowest—the only one under .300—of any player with 50 or more home runs in a year. Johnny Blanchard was the only Yankee to hit two home runs in the 1961 Series; he had hit 21 during the season. The Yankees won the Series from Cincinnati four games to one. Patsy Dougherty of the Boston Red Sox, who hit only 17 home runs in ten seasons in the major leagues (1902-11) was the first to hit two in a World Series game; he connected in the second game of the first World Series in 1903. The Red Sox won the game from Pittsburgh 3-0 and the Series five games to three.

197. Walter (Rabbit) Maranville. Maranville batted .258 in 2670 games over 23 years, 1912-35, with Boston, Pittsburgh, Chicago, Brooklyn and St. Louis in the National League. **198.** Billy Herman. His 67 stolen bases over 15 seasons (1931-47), with several teams, is the lowest total by a Hall of Fame second baseman. **199.** Jimmy Piersall. During his years with the Red Sox between 1950 and 1958, Piersall led the American League in fielding three times. In 1972, Montreal's Ron Fairly had 46 assists, the most by an outfielder in a single season in the 20th century. **200.** Enos Slaughter. Harry Walker hit the single. Joe Frazier (20 in 1954) and Peanuts Lowrey (22 in 1953), both with the Cardinals, were the only players to have 20 or more pinch hits in one year during the 1950s. Los Angeles Dodger Maury Wills, with 94 stolen bases in 1965, was the only man to steal more than 75 in a year in which he failed to hit a home run. Lou Brock is the only player to steal seven bases in a seven-game World Series, and he did it twice. In 1967, he stole seven as the Cardinals beat the Red Sox and in 1968 he did it again as the Cardinals lost to Detroit.

201. Louis Norman (Bobo) Newsom. Over 20 years (1929-53), for many teams, Newsom won 211 and lost 222 games. The other

200-game winner who lost more than he won was Jack Powell. Over 16 seasons (1897–1912), for several teams, Powell won 247 and lost 254. **202.** Bob O'Farrell. As a major league catcher for 21 seasons (1915–35), O'Farrell registered only 1120 hits in 1492 games, the lowest hit total of any non-pitcher who played for 20 years or more. **203.** Denny McLain, 31–6 for the 1968 Detroit Tigers. Charles (Kid) Nichols, 360–202 for three teams over 15 years (1890–1906), was 20 when he won his first game early in the 1890 season, the youngest age at which any 300-game winner recorded his first win. **204.** Wilmer (Vinegar Bend) Mizell. The three pitchers who led the league in losses and strikeouts were: Vic Willis for Boston (National League, 1902), 27–20 overall, 225 strikeouts; Ed Walsh for Chicago (American League, 1911), 27–18 overall, 255 strikeouts; Sam Jones for Chicago (National League, 1955), 14–20 overall, 198 strikeouts. Duane and Herman Pillette were the only father and son combination each to lead the league in losses one year—Herman did it with a 14–19 record for the 1923 Detroit Tigers; Duane did it with a 6–14 year for the 1951 St. Louis Browns.

205. Gordon (Mickey) Cochrane, playing manager of the 1935 Detroit Tigers who beat the Cubs in the World Series four games to two. The Cubs' playing manager was Charlie Grimm who, although on the active roster, did not see any action in the Series. **206.** Bill Dickey of the Yankees; his .362 average in 1936, the highest ever for a catcher, still wasn't good enough for a batting title as Luke Appling hit .388 and Earl Averill hit .378 that year. **207.** Ernie Lombardi. Lombardi won his two batting championships with the Reds in 1938, with a .342 average, and in 1942, with the Braves, with a .330 average. **208.** Al Lopez, who caught more games (1918) than any other catcher in major league history, caught 100 or more games for 12 of his 19 seasons with several teams between 1928 and 1947. Gabby Hartnett of the Cubs also caught 100 or more games for 12 years during his 20-year career, 1922–41.

209. Ray Schalk of the Chicago White Sox. Schalk led American League catchers in putouts for nine years (1913–20, 1922). **210.** Warren (Buddy) Rosar. **211.** Gene Stephens. With the Red Sox, Stephens got three hits in an inning on June 18, 1953. **212.** Pat Seery. He hit four home runs for Chicago against Cleveland on July 18, 1948. His 86 career home runs is the lowest total among players with four in one game. (He played for Cleveland earlier in his career when this picture was taken.)

213. Buddy Myer. **214.** Willie Kamm. **215.** Nellie Fox. Fox struck out only 216 times in 19 seasons with the Athletics, White Sox and Houston (1947–65). **216.** Heinie Groh, National League infielder with the Giants, Reds and Pirates for 16 years (1912–27). At the suggestion of Giant manager John McGraw, Groh developed his "bottle bat" with the handle whittled down to accommodate his small hands. He used it to bat over .300 four times.

217. Boog Powell. **218.** Pittsburgh's Roberto Clemente, born in Carolina, Puerto Rico on August 18, 1934 and killed in an airplane crash on December 31, 1972, became in 1973 the first player born outside the continental United States to be elected to the Hall of Fame. **219.** Larry Doby. During his 13-year career with Cleveland, Chicago and Detroit (1947–59), Doby led the American League in home runs with 32 in 1952 and with 32 again in 1954. He led the league in RBIs with 111 in 1952 and with 121 in 1953, with Cleveland. **220.** Ernie Banks. Banks collected 1009 extra base hits (515 HRs, 407 doubles, 90 triples) during his 19-year career (1953–71), with a .274 lifetime batting average, the lowest career average of any player with 1000 or more extra base hits. In 1966, Baltimore's Frank Robinson had a .316 batting average to go with his league-leading totals of 49 home runs and 122 runs batted in, the lowest average of any triple crown winner. Montreal's Ron Hunt was hit by a record 50 pitches during the 1971 season, breaking the old record of 49 which had been set by Hughie Jennings for Baltimore in the National League in 1896.

INDEX

[Only those people actually shown in the photographs are indexed. The
numbers are those of the photographs.]